A More Excellent Way

L. D. Grant
preacher, teacher, lecturer

Faithful Life Publishers
North Fort Myers, FL

FaithfulLifePublishers.com

A More Excellent Way

© Copyright 2014 by L. D. Grant
ISBN: 978-1-63073-026-0

Published by:
Faithful Life Publishers
North Fort Myers, FL 33903

(888) 720.0950

FaithfulLifePublishers.com
info@FaithfulLifePublishers.com

All Scripture quotations, are taken from the King James Version. All rights reserved. No part of this publication may be reproduced, stored in a retrieval system, or transmitted in any form or by any means — electronic, mechanical, photocopy, recording, or any other — without the permission of the author and/or Faithful Life Publishers.

Printed in the United States of America.

18 17 16 15 14   1 2 3 4 5

Table of Contents

My Heart's Desire 5
My Personal Testimony 7
My Fourfold Purpose 9
My Objectors Answered 10
My Overview Presented..16

SECTION ONE: Scripture Text, Ephesians 4:11-16
    The Gift Of Individuals Given To The Church By God 21
    The Work Of The Gifts Given To The Church By God................31

SECTION TWO: Scripture Text, I Corinthians 1:7, 3:1-3, 12:12, 14:12
    The Unscriptural Exercise By A Church Of The Gifts
        Given To It By God..51
    The Scriptural Evaluation Of The Gifts Given To The
        Church By God 61
    The Fleshly Pursuit Of The Gifts Given To The Church
        By God 71

SECTION THREE: Scripture Text, I Corinthians 12:4-10
    The Nine Gifts Of This Passage Introduced By Paul: 81
      I. Wisdom 85
      II. Knowledge 87
      III. Faith 89
      IV. Divine Healing Presented
          a. Divine Healing Introduced...93
          b. The Three Elements Considered 99
          c. How To Deal With Sickness 107
          d. The Answer To Affliction..117
          e. How To Prolong Cheerfulness 123
          f. Sickness Defined..131
          g. What Is A Sick Person To Do?.................................147
          h. Mutual Healing Sought 157
          i. Three Fallacies About Divine Healing......................163

 V. Divine Miracles.
   Their Definitions, Purpose, Scope, and Duration 171
 VI. Divine Prophecy.
   Its Tests, Purpose, Focus, and Duration 179
 VII. Discerning Of Spirits.
   Its Meaning, Purpose, and Duration 187
 VIII. Divers Kinds Of Tongues.
  a. Tongue Speaking Introduced 191
  b. Is Tongue Speaking Profitable 195
  c. Is Tongue Speaking For Me.......................203
  d. What Are The Rules For and The
    Characteristics Of Tongue Speaking....................211
 IX. Interpretation Of Tongues.
   The Definition, Purpose, Availability, and
   Warning..219

SECTION FOUR: Scripture Text, Romans 12:6-8
 We Have Differing Gifts, But The Same Divine Source 230
 The Differing Gifts Listed and Explained................................231

SECTION FIVE: Scripture Text, I Peter 4:7-11
 The Prerequisites For Those Using Any Gift Properly 237
 The Challenge To Use Each Gift Biblically................................239
 The Rule Over Word and Deed As A Gift Is Used.....................240
 The Godly Results Flowing Out Of The Scriptural
 Use Of Any Gift 241

SECTION SIX: Scripture Text, I Corinthians 13:13
 Abiding Faith 245
 Abiding Hope..246
 Abiding Charity 247

CONCLUSIONS...253
ACKNOWLEDGEMENTS...255
BIBLIOGRAPHY..257

My Heart's Desire

It may not need to be said, but I will say it nevertheless. I write this study with the utmost respect for all those who truly love God, His Word, and His Son, but differ with me doctrinally. I say this because I was raised in a church that practiced many of the doctrines which I will be studying, and bringing under critical examination by the Word of God.

And I must say that as far as I know personally, many of those practicing the doctrines that I shall question lived exemplary personal lives. Why they differed doctrinally with me, I cannot say exactly. In fact, some lived more godly lives, in the everyday sense, than those who agreed with me doctrinally. Thus I now have concluded that DOCTRINE must be known, believed, and then practiced faithfully before we shall see that ONE FAITH lived by everyone who professes to know Jesus Christ as Savior and Lord.

I therefore desire to know the truth for Biblical truth will set me free: *"and you shall know the truth, and the truth shall make you free,"* John 8:32.* Oh, I trust this will be the desire of your heart also for I long to see everyone free to serve God!

In the Service of the King,

Rev. L. D. Grant

*All Bible references will be taken from the
AUTHORIZED KING JAMES VERSION.

My Personal Testimony

I'd rather walk daily hand-in-hand with Jesus, having no gift at all, than to be able to exercise all of the gifts mentioned in the Bible, and not have His hand in mine.

He is more precious to me than any gift I could receive from him since He is my "unspeakable gift," II Corinthians 9:15. He is my all-sufficiency for I know that when I have a right relationship with Him that He'll supply my every need; therefore I do not need anything beyond what He has ordained that I should have. In fact, if I do desire anything beyond what He wills to give to me—I Sin Grievously Against Him! I also insult Him by saying, in effect, that His presence is not sufficient for me, and that His daily provision for me is inadequate.

I therefore will be content with God's will for my life, for then and only then will I be satisfied, happy, and fulfilled while I'm here on earth, and eventually receive all the heavenly rewards my Lord desires to give to me in the future.

But you say, what then should I do? The answer is simple: walk daily with the Lord, and He will give you EVERYTHING you need to do His will for your life. This is the More Excellent Way the Apostle Paul is talking about:

"But covet earnestly the best gifts: and yet show I unto you a more excellent way," I Corinthians 12:31.

For years, far too many believers have argued, and even fought over whether the gifts were only for the first century, or whether they are still available to us today. However, in doing this they have been missing the main message of this passage: there is A MORE EXCELLENT WAY available to believers whether they lived in the first century, or in any other century from that time until the end of time! Having a right relationship with God through my Lord Jesus Christ I have the potential to live my life according to the good and perfect will of God.

Now, honestly, who could ask for anything more than that? When God is put first, we seek only His good and perfect will for our lives even if it consists of only being a faithful everyday child of God. Have you ever considered seriously this possibility? Please do it now! I say this because our heavenly rewards will not be based on how many gifts we have had while on earth, but whether we did the will of God while we were on planet earth!

Now lest I should be misunderstood from the beginning let me say that I APPROVE OF THE SCRIPTURAL USAGE OF EVERY GIFT THAT GOD HAS GIVEN TO THE CHURCH. However, I must hasten to say that I also believe that the Apostle Paul introduces us to A More Excellent Way in I Corinthians 12:31. We'll be talking about that concept throughout our study.

On the other hand, let me say, that I am adamantly against the unscriptural usage of any gift that God has given to the Church. In the following material I will make three statements expressing just how adamant I am against the unscriptural usage of any of the gifts God has given to the Church. The gifts are too precious to be misused!

Anyone using any gift from God to elevate his own supposed spirituality before men is abusing the gift, is deceiving himself, is misleading God's people, and is robbing God of the honor and glory that are rightfully His.

Anyone using any gift from God to feather his own nest is misusing the gift, is hoodwinking himself, is robbing God's people, and is insulting the God who gave the gift to the Church. Thus I believe the hottest spot in Hell/the Lake of Fire will be reserved for those who pretend to use the gifts God has given to the Church to rob the rich, the poor, the destitute, the feeble in body and mind, and those in desperate need to make themselves rich. Yes, they have a right to the basic needs of life, but to live above a modest manner is to demonstrate just how little respect they have for those they are fleecing.

Anyone using any gift from God to advance his own agenda is improperly using the gift, is taking advantage of God's people, and is laying himself open to judgment by Almighty God.

The gifts given to the Church are too sacred to be mishandled by anyone; therefore it behooves each handler to know how to use each gift Biblically. I must never arrogantly belittle the gifts given by God to the Church. I must never purposefully misuse the gifts given to the Church by God. However, I must continually give proper respect to the gifts, and make sure that I use the gifts Scripturally—THEY ARE GIFTS FROM GOD TO THE CHURCH!

My Fourfold Purpose:

I have written this book in the following manner so that it can fulfill a fourfold purpose.

First, it can be easily understood by anyone willing to study carefully its contents.

Secondly, it can be readily taught with little or no further study. The outline form makes this possible.

Thirdly, it can be quickly preached since the outline is already sermon ready.

Fourthly, it can be developed by any competent scholar who wishes to go deeper into the Word as it relates to the subject at hand.

Yes, I know that the readability element is missing. However, just think, the points are already laid out so you do not have to dig them out. My prayer is that whoever picks up this book will be blessed by it regardless of whatever spiritual level he/she may be on at that time.

I have also written out many of the Scripture references used since I know my own tendency not to look up references that seem to be familiar to me. In doing this I have, no doubt, missed entirely the focal point the writer had in his mind, and I have failed to give the Holy Spirit the opportunity to teach me personally what the references had to say to me. I trust that this policy will be the source of many blessings to you.

My Objectors Answered:

Now before we begin to study the Biblical passages that are related to the subject before us, I want to deal with some very elementary problems we need to overcome before we begin our in-depth study of our subject. I'm doing this so that we'll all be on the same page as we study. First, I trust that we will come to this study accepting the Bible as the inspired and infallible Word of God!

> *"All scripture is given by inspiration of God, and is profitable for doctrine, for reproof, for correction, for instruction in righteousness: That the man of God may be perfect, thoroughly furnished unto all good works,"* II Timothy 3:16, 17.

Next, I trust that we'll accept what the Bible has to say to us like the church folks did at the church in Thessalonica:

> *"For this cause also thank we God without ceasing, because, when ye received the word of God which ye heard of us, ye received it not as the word of men, but as it is in truth, the word of God, which effectually worketh also in you that believe,"* I Thessalonians 2:13.

And lastly, I want us all to allow the Holy Spirit to lead us unto all truth:

> *"Howbeit when he, the Spirit of truth, is come, he will guide you into all truth: for he shall not speak of himself, but whatsoever he shall hear, that shall he speak: and he will show you things to come,"* John 16:13.

Are you still with me? Will you pray with me that we will allow the Holy Spirit to lead us? I'll be eternally thankful to you if you will?

Now I'm going to list the seven most frequently stated objections that have, and will keep us from doing what we have prayed will happen.

1. We hear from many that God did not say this or that in the Bible. In other words it is the product of man's ingenuity, not God's inspiration. Please refer back to our II Timothy 3:16, 17 passage, then add II Peter 1:20, 21.

"Knowing this first, that no prophecy of the scripture is of any private interpretation. For prophecy came not in old time by the will of man: but holy men of God spake as they were moved by the Holy Ghost."

If these two passages are not enough to convince you that the Bible is God's Holy Word, then neither would a hundred more.

2. We hear from others that God did say it, but He did not mean it. This makes God a lair, which He is not. Notice the three following verses:

"God is not a man, that he should lie; neither the son of man, that he should repent: hath he said, and shall he not do it? Or hath he spoken, and shall he not make it good," Numbers 23:19.

"In hope of eternal life, which God, that cannot lie, promised before the world began," Titus 1:2.

"That by two immutable things, in which it was impossible for God to lie, we might have a strong consolation, who have fled for refuge to lay hold upon the hope set before us," Hebrews 6:18.

But there is one who is the father of every lie:

"Ye are of your Father the devil, and the lusts of your father ye will do. He was a murderer from the beginning, and abode not in the truth, because there is no truth in him. When he speaketh a lie he speaketh of his own: for he is a lair, and the father of it," John 8:44.

Thus in every doctrinal statement there is only one Biblical truth. I am under a holy obligation to find it, and so are you!

3. Next, we hear from those who feel that they are in a category all by themselves believing that God indeed said it and meant it, but it did not refer to them. What part doesn't, and how will I know which part does and which part does not? It either ALL applies to everyone addressed, or it doesn't apply to anyone who is addressed! When the Bible says, *"So then every one of us*

shall give account of himself to God," does it apply to everyone, someone, or no one, Romans 14:12? The very Words of Jesus shall judge us: *"He that rejecteth me, and receiveth not my words hath one that judgeth him: the word that I have spoken, the same shall judge him in the last day,"* John 12:48.

4. Fourthly, we look at those who say that they believe every Word in the Bible, but they have received further revelation from God that sheds new light on hitherto unknown teaching from God.

Please remember that God's Word is established in heaven forever, Psalm 119:89.

"For ever, O Lord, thy word is settled in heaven."

Next remember that God does not change, Malachi 3:6a.

"For I am the Lord, I change not..."

And finally notice that God warns us not to add to His Word, nor take away from it:

"Ye shall not add unto the word which I command you, neither shall ye diminish aught from it...," Deuteronomy 4:2.

"Only be thou strong and very courageous, that thou mayest observe to do according to all the law, which Moses my servant commandeth thee: turn not from it to the right hand or to the left, that thou mayest prosper withersoever thou goest," Joshua 1:7.

"For I testify unto every man that heareth the words of the prophecy of this book, If any man shall add unto these things, God shall add unto him the plagues that are written in this book: and if any man shall take away from the words of the book of this prophecy, God shall take away his part out of the book of life, and out of the holy city, and from the things which are written in this book," Revelation 22:18, 19.

And although each warning is directly tied to the immediate passage where it is found, this we would readily admit, yet the principle is still crystal clear—do not add to, nor take away from the Word of God for it is our only all-sufficient guide as it relates to our faith and practice both now and forever! God's Word is to be taken exactly as it is given. No man could ever improve upon it in any way. NO MAN, EVER!

5. Fifthly, certain objectors inform me that there have been times when God has winked at certain practices forbidden by Him, and that now is one of those times. If that is true, then it is also the time when God has commanded all men everywhere to repent.

"And the times of this ignorance God winked at; but now commandeth all men every where to repent," Acts 17:30.

I would also exhort you to read chapters two and three of the book of Revelation to find out what God has to say to the churches about adhering to what the Bible has to say to them.

6. Sixthly, I frequently hear that the Bible is old fashion, out-of-date, and needs to be updated. If the Word of God is *"settled for ever in heaven"* as Psalm 119:89 says that it is, and if *"not one jot or tittle shall pass from the law until all of it be fulfilled"* as Matthew 5:18 informs us, then no update is needed now, it has never needed to be updated in the past, and it certainly will not need to be updated in the future. Yes, *"heaven and earth shall pass away,"* but the Word stands forever!

7. The last objection I hear is: but we have and we will accomplish far more through our efforts, our programs, and our methods than Could Ever Be Attempted by those who follow the Bible to the letter. It is then voiced in the heart, or verbally, I challenge you to compare what we have done, what we are now doing, and what we are planning to do to Your Efforts in the same areas. And I do that with an honest and open heart! I also make sure that I praise God for every effort that has brought Him the honor and praise that are due unto His glorious name. However, I often read Matthew 7:21-23 slowly and prayerfully, then pray: "Oh dear God, I ask in the name of Jesus that I will be found doing only those things which are ordained by God, under the

superintendence of the Holy Spirit, and for God's honor and glory." Would you pray that prayer with me? Then meditate much on the passage before us.

"Not every one that saith unto me, Lord, Lord, shall enter into the kingdom of heaven, but he that doeth the will of my Father which is in heaven. Many will say to me in that day, Lord, Lord, have we not prophesied in thy name? and in thy name cast out devils? and in thy name done many wonderful works. And then will I profess unto them, I never knew you:depart from me, ye that work iniquity."

You see there must always be a Biblical balance between Truth on the one hand, and the Spirit on the other hand. This pertains to worship as well as any and every effort pertaining to service. Jesus sets forth this truth in John 4:24, *"God is a spirit: and they that worship him must worship him in spirit and in truth."*

Truth sets forth the correct information about God that the Holy Spirit needs to cause my spirit to respond in true worship of God.

All truth and no Spirit leads to dead or apparently dead orthodoxy, and too much Spirit without enough truth to guide it leads to fanaticism. The Holy Spirit always works in light of what the Word teaches, but the Word needs the Holy Spirit to teach us what the Word means, and how we are to respond to what the Word teaches. There is never a conflict between the Word and the Spirit who gave the Word. If He carried along (φερόμενοι) the Scripture writers He is certainly able to teach us what he inspired them to write.

Now I must openly admit that I have, at times, under-empathized the importance of the ministry of the Holy Spirit in my daily life and in my ministry. This has sometimes led to a real or perceived dead orthodoxy. I've been letter perfect, but spiritually deficient. On the other hand perhaps you have over-empathized the importance of the Holy Spirit in your daily life, and maybe even in your ministry. This may have caused you to have some or all of the problems we have mentioned thus far. It may have also led some into fanaticism. May I therefore suggest that we both make sure that we keep a proper Biblical balance between the Word and the Spirit, then our combined efforts will be focused on seeking only God's will.

Listen very carefully to what the Apostle Paul has to say to the believers at Corinth, I Corinthians 12:31:

> *"But covet earnestly the best gifts: and yet shew I unto you a more excellent way."*

Now literally translated from the Greek text of Stephens, 1550a.d. it reads *"Be emulous (Ζηλοῦτε) of but the gifts better, and yet more surpassing (Καθ' ὑπερβολὴν) a way to you I shew."* The word translated covet or emulous means to be striving to equal or to excel and the word translated more excellent refers to that which greatly exceeds others. Thus Paul tells the Corinthians to seek to equal the better gifts, but they should realize that in doing this they will not ever reach the exalted status that they could when they fully understand how far his More Excellent Way exceeds their efforts relating to the better gifts!

Now Paul's exhortation to covet the better gifts cannot ever be Scripturally realized through the efforts of the flesh, but must be fulfilled through the More Excellent Way he will expound unto us while dealing with all the gifts mentioned in the Scriptural passages he has used relating to this subject. However, the process can be summarized in the following words: so live your life that the end product will be a person who is found in the center of God's will receiving from the Holy Spirit each and every gift he needs to do that good and perfect will of God for his life.

I do not know about you, but I want to learn all I can about this MORE EXCELLENT WAY. It is God's daily provision that is obtained by walking with God, doing His will, and living a Holy life in accordance with the truth revealed through His Word and His Spirit. This guarantees me EVERYTHING I need everyday I live to do all that God asks of me. This is the More Excellent Way Paul wants to show unto us. Amen?

Just remember that on the darkest day of your life, even when you do not have a single gift to exercise, that you have Jesus, the Bible, and the Holy Spirit. Jesus has promised to *"never leave thee, nor forsake thee. So that we may boldly say, The Lord is my helper,"* Hebrews 13:5c, 6a. The Holy Spirit who indwells us, I Corinthians 6:19, will help our infirmities so that we can pray as we ought, Romans 8:26, 27. And the Word of God gives us the faith we need to go on, Romans 8:28, 10:17. Now honestly, do you need more than is offered to you in these verses?

My Overview Presented

I believe that it is now time for me to give you an overview of the gifts we are getting ready to study. I exhort you to study it carefully since it lays out the whole picture on one page, and it summarizes all the material to be studied. There are six different passages before us, but you'll notice that even though they are related (they all deal with gifts), yet each passage has its own particular distinctions. Even a cursory study of this overview should cause you to see how the passages compliment one another so that when studied thoroughly you have a complete picture of their source, their usage, and their importance. May God aid you in your study of this overview. I have listed all of the information under six headings so that we can focus more clearly. In all we will look at twenty-four categories of gifts before we finish this study. I'll be using six main passages of Scripture that deal with the gifts and their usage. Thus we are undertaking a very large task as we do this. However, if you will take the time to familiarize yourself with this overview it will greatly increase your ability to understand, and then use it profitably.

A GENERAL OVERVIEW OF THE GIFTS

Their Individual Identity	Their Scriptural Hierarchy	Their Divine Source	Their Proper Use	Their Specific Use	Their Abiding Nature
5 categories	8 categories	9 categories	7 categories	1 categories	3 categories
Acts 4:11	I Corinthians 12:28, 29	I Corinthians 12:8-11	Romans 12:6-8	I Peter 4:8-11	I Corinthians 13:13
apostles	apostles				
prophets	prophets	prophecy	prophecy		
evangelists					
pastors					
teachers	teachers		teaching		
	miracles	miracles			
	healings				
	helps				
	governments				
	tongues	tongues			
		wisdom			
		knowledge			
		faith			faith
		healings			
		discerning of spirits			
		interpretation of tongues			
			ministry		
			exhorteth		
			giveth		
			ruleth		
			mercy		
				stewards	
					hope
					charity

Now that you have perused this overview page I would ask you to please remember that as awesome and beneficial as the gifts are that they are to be used by the saints of God as either a sign to the unbeliever (I Corinthians 14:22) or as the means: "For the perfecting of the saints, for the work of the ministry, for the edifying of the body of Christ" (Ephesians 4:12). And unless we learn to use these gifts under the superintendence of the Holy Spirit (whether He gives them directly or whether He chooses to use our God given natural talents) we shall never obtain the unity which should exist within the body of Christ, Ephesians 4:3-6.

What an awe inspiring scene this could be: The Church totally submitted unto Jesus Christ as its Head, the saints of God united in heart, soul, and mind as it relates to the cause of Christ, and the unbelieving world shaken to its core as the armies of God spread the glorious Gospel of Jesus Christ to the ends of the earth! IT CAN BE DONE! WILL YOU HELP ME DO IT? THEN BEGIN NOW TO STUDY IN EARNEST WITH ME THE FOLLOWING MATERIAL.

SECTION ONE

Scripture Text: Ephesians 4:11-16

Scripture Text: Ephesians 4:11.

Title: The Gift Of Individuals Given To The Church By God.

Theme: A More Excellent Way.

Introduction: We are now ready to make the transition from the introductory material to the meat of our study. We begin by focusing upon the Individuals God Has Given To The Church. I read in Ephesians 4:11, *"and he gave some apostles, and some prophets, and some evangelists, and some pastors and teachers."* The he is God in this context. It is He who has given these five categories of gifts to the church for its perfection. It is incumbent upon us therefore to know all we can about the gifts God has given to us so that we can do the work, and will of God to His honor and glory throughout the Church Age.

If we are called and gifted to be one of those individuals we must minister as God would have us to serve. But if we are not called and gifted to be one of these individuals, then we must respond to their ministry so that we grow up in the Lord. Since God does all things well, we cannot improve upon His plan, ever!

Let us therefore humbly seek to understand, and do that good and perfect will of God. Amen?

I. THE GIFT OF INDIVIDUALS GIVEN TO THE CHURCH BY GOD, Ephesians 4:ll.

(All the Greek words used in this book will be taken from the ENGLISHMAN'S GREEK NEW TESTAMENT, and all of the definitions and parsing of verbs will be taken from HARPER'S ANALYTICAL GREEK LEXICON.)

A. Apostles, ἀποστόλους.

1. The original twelve apostles were chosen by Jesus, Luke 6:13-16.

2. However, Matthias was chosen by the one hundred twenty disciples, and the eleven apostles who were gathered in the upper room to replace Judas, Acts 1:15, 25, 26.

3. Paul introduces himself to a number of churches as one called to be an apostle, Romans 1:1.

4. Jesus Christ is called "the Apostle and High Priest of our profession," Hebrew 3:1.

5. The basic meaning of this word refers to one sent on a mission.

6. The apostles were sent by God on the divine mission of laying the foundation for His Church. The prophets were also involved in this mission, "And are built upon the foundation of the apostles and prophets, Jesus Christ being the chief corner stone," Ephesians 2:20.

7. After the death of Jesus to be an apostle a man had to "measure up" to certain requirements which were laid down in Acts, chapter one.
    a. He had to accompany Jesus from His baptism unto His ascension, Acts 1:21, 22a.
    b. He had to be ordained to be a witness with the eleven of Jesus' resurrection, Acts 1:22b.
    c. He had to be selected by the eleven other apostles, as well as the one hundred twenty disciples, Acts 1:26b.

8. Their office was set aside when their mission was fulfilled.
    a. Thus we do not have apostles, apostolic succession, nor apostolic authority today.
    b. But you say, what about the Apostle Paul?
        1.) |He was commissioned personally by Jesus, Acts 9:6, Galatians 1:1, I Timothy 2:7.
        2.) And he had seen the resurrected Lord, I Corinthians 15:8.

    c. I have never been able to find anyone in my lifetime that could meet the requirements necessary to be called an apostle. And I do not know of anyone who has ever met such an individual either, that is, since the New Testament days.

B. Prophets, προφήτας.

  1. We have sixteen writing prophets (4 major and 12 minor) in the Old Testament and a number of speaking prophets.

    a. Both speaking and writing prophets are quoted in the New Testament.

    b. Examples: Elijah, I Kings 19:1 and James 5:17; Isaiah 7:14 and Matthew 1:22.

  2. We have five prophets named in the New Testament.

    a. Barnabas, Acts 13:1, I Corinthians 9:1-6.

    b. Judas and Silas, Acts 15:32.

    c. Agabus, Acts 21:10.

    d. Jesus, Luke 24:19.

  3. We also have at least five prophetesses mentioned in the Bible, and five virgins who prophesied.

    a. However, none of these spoke or wrote any prophecies that had New Testament Church pertinence.

    b. They were: Miriam, Exodus 15:20; Deborah, Judges 4:4; Huldah, II Kings 22:14; Noadiah, Nehemiah, 6:14; Anna, Luke 2:36.

    c. The four daughters of Philip, the evangelist, did prophesy, but we have nothing of which they said, Acts 21:9.

  4. The ministry of the prophets, whether in the Old Testament or the New Testament, was twofold.

    a. There was a foretelling of future events informing the people of their day what God was going to do in the future.

1.) Some of their prophecies are yet to be fulfilled, such as, the coming Day of the Lord.

2.) We still preach about these prophecies, but we do not prophesy in the sense of foretelling.

b. There was a forth telling of the present relating how God's people in particular, and sinners in general had broken God's laws, what the penalty would be if they continued in their sin, their need to repent, and the forgiveness God would give to those who repented.

c. In one sense of the term all the New Testament writers are writing prophets: they give revelation relating to future events and they challenge sinners to repent while exhorting the saints to live holy lives just like their Old Testament counterparts did.

d. Their office ceased when revelation was completed, I Corinthians 13:8-10.

1.) We read in I Corinthians 13:8b, "but whether there be prophecies, they shall fail," no more prophecies shall be given for God has given us all the prophecies we will ever need.

2.) This passage can be translated, they shall be done away, καταργηθήσοντι.

3.) Prophecy was in part for the New Testament when these verses were written, 56 or 57a.d.

4.) Yet to be written were at least: Luke, John, Acts, Ephesians, Philippians, Colossians, I and II Timothy, Titus, Philemon, Hebrews, I and II Peter, I, II, and III John, and Revelation.

5.) The part (μέρους) we read about in I Corinthians 13:9, 10 was done away with when the whole (τέλειον) was completed.

e. The Bible deals with redemptive truth, and I have all the redemptive truth I need contained in my Bible both now, and forever for it is established in heaven for all of eternity, Psalm 119:89.

    f. Thus I ask you to introduce me to a prophet who can meet the acid test laid down by God for a prophet, Deuteronomy 18:22, "When a prophet speakesth in the name of the Lord, if the thing follow not, nor come to pass, that is the thing which the Lord hath not spoken, but the prophet hath spoken it presumptuously: thou shalt not be afraid of him." God also laid a very heavy penalty upon those who spoke in His name when He did not command them to do so, "But the prophet, which shall presume to speak a word in my name, which I have not commanded him to speak, or that shall speak in the name of other gods, even that prophet shall die," Deuteronomy 18:20.

    g. The prophets of the Old Testament and the New Testament combined their God given efforts to lay the foundation for the New Testament Church so that we could build on it a glorious superstructure, Jesus Christ, being the chief corner stone, "And are built upon the foundation of the apostles and prophets, Jesus Christ himself being the chief corner stone," Ephesians 2:20.

C. Evangelists, εὐαγγελιστάς.

1. Once the prophets and the apostles laid the foundation of the Church the Chief Cornerstone ordained three classes of individuals to direct the building upon that foundation.

2. One of these classes is called evangelists.

3. And within that one class called evangelists we find that three categories of people can do what we call the work of an evangelist.

    a. Philip evidently was a fulltime evangelist, Acts 21:8. We still have fulltime evangelists today, but they are fewer in number than ever before in my lifetime. They hold special meetings in local churches or citywide campaigns that usually last from three days to extended periods.

b. Timothy, a pastor, was told to do the work of an evangelist by the Apostle Paul, II Timothy 4:5.

I have held evangelistic meetings as a pastor for other local church pastors. Let me relate one such experience. It occurred on a stormy wintry week in November while I was holding evangelistic meetings in a small town southwest of Springfield, Illinois. We had great services on Sunday and the weather was fair, but on Monday it was foggy, wet, and windy.

As I drove up to the church I thought no one would be there. Was I ever surprised to see the church packed! God gave complete freedom as I preached, and when I gave the invitation it seemed that, at least, one-third of those there came forward. The pastor stopped leading the invitational hymn so that he could direct the soul winners. Someone immediately took over his job leading the invitational hymns. Then the pianist stopped playing the piano, went to her daughter who came forward with her, and they both were reconciled with God and one another. Another lady took over the piano playing, and the invitation time continued on until almost everyone was either at the altar or helping those who were.

Every time of think of that night I rejoice in the Lord that He had allowed me to do the work of an evangelist. But I also do the work of an evangelist when I go soul winning, usually on an individual basis.

c. And those believers who were scattered abroad by persecution went everywhere evangelizing (εὐαγγελιζόμενοι), Acts 8:4. In other words they were sharing the glad tidings about salvation through faith in Jesus Christ. Every believer should be involved in this type of evangelism.

4. After all, this is the basic meaning of the Word.
   5. So long as there is a Church the position of the evangelist will be needed. This will be set forth later as we look at the Work Of The Individuals Who Are Gifts Unto The Church.
D. Pastors, ποιμένας.
   1. Pastors are involved in the local church ministries, I Peter 5:2a.
   2. They are the under-shepherds working directly under the Chief Shepherd's leadership, I Peter 5:4. Thus Jesus Christ will determine their rebukes or rewards!
   3. They basically have the responsibility of shepherding and feeding the flock of God, I Peter 5:2, John 21:15-17.
   4. Their qualifications are set forth in I Timothy 3:1-8, I Peter 5:2, 3, Titus 1:5-9.
   5. From Pentecost until the rapture occurs local churches will need godly pastors.
   6. Godly pastors are willing to sacrifice continually for the work of the Lord, Philippians 2:17.
E. Teachers, διδασκάλους.
   1. Jesus Christ was a teacher, John 3:2.
   2. The Apostle Paul was a teacher, I Timothy 2:7.
   3. Teachers are gifts from God, Ephesians 4:11.
   4. Teachers hold the third highest ranking among the gifts which were given, I Corinthians 12:28.
   5. Teachers shall receive the greater judgment, James 3:1 (be not many masters/teachers, διδασκάλοι).
   6. The basic meaning of this word is to impart divine truth in such a manner that it is absorbed and practiced.
      a. Thus we can teach by word and by example.
      b. But the Biblical teacher is always involved in imparting divine truth.

7. A teacher can do the work of an evangelist, and the work of a pastor. A pastor can teach and do the work of an evangelist. And an evangelist can both teach and preach.

There are some extremely important points I yet need to deal with before we go on with our in-depth study of our subject.

1. These five categories of individuals were given ('ἔδωκεν) as gifts (δόματα) to men, Ephesians 4:8. However, I see in I Corinthians 12:28 that three of them (apostles, prophets, and teachers) were set in the assembly ('ἐκκλησία) by God.

2. Thus these gifts given by God to the Church were not obtained by man, but were given by God to man.

3. I cite the example of the Apostle Paul:

   a. He could legitimately say I am gifted in all five categories.
   1.) Paul was a teacher, Acts 18:11.

   2.) Paul was a pastor, Acts 19:9, 10.

   3.) Paul was an evangelist, Acts 20:7.

   4.) Paul was an apostle, Galatians 1:1.

   5.) Paul was a writing prophet, I Thessalonians 4:13-18.

   b. And he could Scripturally say that he was given these gifts by God. Notice the following passages:
   1.) An apostle, not of men, neither by man, but through the Lord Jesus Christ, Galatians 1:1.

   2.) He was a called apostle, Romans 1:1.

   3.) He was ordained a preacher, an apostle, and a teacher, I Timothy 2:7.

   4.) He was commanded by Jesus Christ to be an apostle, I Timothy 1:1.

   5.) He was an apostle by the will of God, II Corinthians 1:1.

4. Man therefore should not try to promote himself to any one of these offices, he must be called by God, Acts 20:28.

5. I CITE TWO PASSAGES TO SHOW YOU HOW GREAT THE PRESSURE IS WHEN YOU ARE IN THE MINISTRY, Acts 15:37, 38, II Timothy 4:10.

   a. Acts 15:38 speaks of Mark who *"went not with them to the work."* This suggests that his immaturity got the best of him at that time. After some seasoning he became profitable in the ministry.

   b. II Timothy 4:10 tells us that Demas *"hath forsaken me, having loved this present world..."* Evidently, he loved the world more than he loved the work of the Lord.

   c. You need a definite call from God to withstand the pressures that come upon you as a servant of God.

   d. And you need it also for you own self-assurance.

   e. My personal testimony is that I received a definite call to the ministry about two o'clock in the morning while I was proving a new oil pumping station near Rockport, Indiana. God spoke very definitely to my heart using John 21:15-17. That call has kept me always on the right tract, generally in the right frame of mind, and in the place of blessing during my years of preparation and ministry. When all else and everyone else failed me that call to shepherd His sheep and feed His lambs and sheep kept me in the center of His will for my life. Without that call I would have surely fallen many times. Oh, how I praise Him for that definite call!

Now you may not believe that a definite call is needed to serve in one or more of these five areas listed in Ephesians 4:11, but I do. Thus you and I will answer to God one day as to which was the correct Biblical position. May we both arrive at the one that pleases God! As for me I am going to rely on the Holy Spirit to separate those God chooses to use for His work, Acts 13:2, 20:28; Hebrews 5:4, 5.

"As they ministered to the Lord, and fasted, the Holy Ghost said, Separate me Barnabas and Saul for the work whereunto I have called them," Acts 13:2.

"Take heed therefore unto yourselves, and to all the flock, over the which the Holy Ghost hath made you overseers, to feed the church of God, which he hath purchased with his own blood," Acts 20:28.

"And no man taketh this honour unto himself, but he that is called of God as was Aaron. So also Christ glorified not himself to be made an high priest; but he that said unto him, Thou art my Son, today have I begotten thee," Hebrews 5:4, 5.

Having laid bare my heart, it is now time for us to begin to study The Work of the Individuals Given to the Church by God as Gifts.

Scripture Text: Ephesians 4:12-16.

Theme: A More Excellent Way.

Title: The Work of the Individuals Given to the Church by God.

Introduction: In verse eleven of our text we are told that God gave certain gifts to the Church. Now these gifts were not talents, but individuals who had certain abilities because they had received a definite call from God. Each area seems to be a distinct area. Some were temporary (apostles, prophets), and some were permanent (evangelists, pastors, teachers). And some seem to overlap in some areas: a pastor can teach and do evangelistic work, a teacher can pastor and do evangelistic work, and an evangelist can pastor and teach. Now these gifts were given unto the Church with a definite purpose in mind: that it might be perfected through the proper use of these gifts. It is therefore incumbent upon the Church to receive these gifts in a godly manner so that it could fulfill its high and holy calling. Let us then center our thoughts upon the purpose of the gifts.

II. THE WORK OF THE INDIVIDUALS GIVEN TO THE CHURCH BY GOD AS GIFTS.

   A. The Purpose Of The Gifts Given To The Church By God.

      1. For the perfecting of the saints.

         a. God gives evangelists, pastors, and teachers as gifts to local churches, did you know that?

         b. God has given evangelists, pastors, and teachers the tremendous job of perfecting the saints in His Church.

            1.) That's an awesome responsibility laid upon the evangelists, the pastors, and the teachers, Hebrews 13:17b.

            2.) But it is a holy obligation on the church's part to receive the gifts that God has given to it, Hebrews 13:17 a, c.

         c. The word perfected means to restore a thing to its proper place, and then make it complete, καταρτισμόν.

1.) Man's proper place is walking with God always with all of his heart.

2.) But man is totally depraved, thus he walks amiss, Isaiah 53:6.

3.) However, he becomes a new creation in Christ the moment he is saved, II Corinthians 5:17.

4.) And from that moment on he should be working on perfecting his life, Ephesians 2:8-10.

5.) This is why we have various church services in our churches—to perfect you!

6.) I used the following program to round out the whole man in each church I pastured. Sunday School was used to share the Word of God with all the students so that there could be an increase in faith, Romans 10:17. The Morning Worship service was used to give opportunity for all to worship God in Spirit and in Truth, John 4:23, 24. The Evening Service was used to give repose for the mind, spirit, and soul, Psalm 73. And the Wednesday Evening service was used for in-dept studies of the Word of God, II Tim. 2:15.

d. It takes time for the perfecting of the saints.

1.) The perfecting comes from the contact with the men of God who have been in contact with God.

2.) The spiritual man avails himself to the gifts of God, and receives all that is needed for his perfection.

3.) Perfecting can come by forsaking sin or by growing in grace or both.

4.) How much time do you spend perfecting yourself? Are you more faithful now than last year? Have you matured in the Lord this last year? Is your devotional life richer now? Have you put into practice what the evangelist, your pastor, and your teacher have shared with you?

2. For the work of the ministry, 'έγον διακονίας.
   a. The work of the ministry is a most difficult work for the following reasons:
      1.) You cannot fire those who are not being perfected even though they steadfastly resist your efforts to perfect them.
      2.) You cannot force anyone to be perfected even though you can vividly see their need.
      3.) You can only preach, teach, exhort, encourage, and pray that they will be perfected.
      4.) But how grievous it is to God to see such great potential being wasted because it is not being perfected through His gifts to the Church.
   b. This is why a man must have the call and the gift to be an evangelist, to pastor a church, or to teach.
      1.) Without God he will utterly fail.
      2.) A man may have only one or he may have all three gifts in this area, but he must use properly what he has.
      3.) What he has is what you need for your perfecting. Please never forget that!
3. For the edifying of the Body of Christ.
   a. To edify (οἰκοδομὴν) means to make strong in the Lord.
   b. The body (σώματος) refers to the believers who are in Christ, Colossians 1:18, *"And he is the head of the body, the church: who is the beginning, the firstborn from the dead; that in all things he might have the preeminence."*
   c. An evangelist is to challenge each hearer, the pastor is to edify each believer in Christ, and the teacher is to instruct each student; therefore you are responsible to hear every sermon, every message, and every lesson proclaimed by them that God has ordained for you to hear.
      1.) When God burdens their hearts, it is for your perfection because God knows what you need.

2.) If you fail to listen you have missed some lesson on how you could be perfected.

3.) God wants them to exercise you spiritually so that you will be strong in Him.

4.) How strong are you in Him, right now?

5.) How often do you exercise?

B. The Duration Of The Gifts Given To The Church By God.

1. Till we all come unto the unity of the faith.

   a. God says that these gifts will remain until we ALL come unto the unity of the faith. We are certainly not there yet! Are we? And we will not be until He comes!

   b. There is only one true faith, Ephesians 4:5.

   c. You see how great a job these three gifts have before God?

   d. They must unite the believers in Christ so that they all think like God, act like God, and speak like God. Romans 10:17, informs us how we can have the full faith we need to do this.

   e. Then the Body of Christ will function as one united whole with Jesus Christ as its head, Colossians 1:15-18.

2. Till we are all come unto the knowledge of the Son.

   a. God looks into your hearts, sees what knowledge you lack, and then He moves in the hearts of those He has gifted so that they share that knowledge with you. In doing this He will share the whole council of God with you.

   b. Thus you learn more and more about Jesus! The second stanza of the song, More About Jesus should be the song of each believer's heart. *"More about Jesus let me learn, More of His holy will discern; Spirit of God, my teacher be, Showing the things of Christ to me." LIVING HYMNS, stanza two, page 482.*

c. Doctrine must be taught faithfully, then lived diligently, and finally shared exactly.
3. Till we all come unto the perfect man.
   a. Is there anyone perfect? Then, there is much work yet to be done by those gifted and those needing the gifts.
   b. Our goal in life should be perfection in Christ, not conformity unto the world, Romans 12:1, 2.
   c. I love to feed the babes in Christ the Word of God. The congregation in Olympia, Brazil sat like baby birds looking for mother's return with a worm in her mouth because their hunger for the Word was so great. What a privilege it was to feed them with God's precious Word!
   d. But I love also to feed the mature ones in Christ the meat of the Word. God gives us three kinds of spiritual food to feast upon in the Word: I Peter 2:2-milk, I Corinthians 3:2-meat, Hebrews 5:14-strong meat.
4. Till we all reach the measure of the stature of the fullness of Christ.
   a. Christ is our example, Romans 8:29.
   b. Our fullness will never be full this side of heaven, but we should be as full as is humanly possible.

C. The Necessity Of The Gifts Given To The Church By God.
  1. That stability is produced in the Body of Christ.
     a. That we henceforth (μηκέτι--no longer).
        1.) This strongly implies that until we as pastors, teachers, evangelists, and you, the people of God, put into practice what is being taught here—we will be tossed to and fro by every wind of doctrine.
        2.) But it is even more strongly implied that when everyone addressed in this passage puts into practice what is being taught, then and only then, will God's people be no longer tossed to and fro by every wind of doctrine.

3.) Thus, growth must be experienced until we move out of our infancy, as it pertains to our Christian faith, unto full maturity in Christ.

b. Be no more children (νήπιοι-infants or those unlearned).

1.) Infants are controlled by those who exert the strongest influence upon them.

2.) They are not able to resist outside pressures which control their every move.

3.) In like manner, those who are in the infancy stage of their Christian life will be easily controlled by those who are stronger than they are.

c. Tossed to and fro (κλυδωνιζόμενοι--as waves move about).

1.) An infant will be taught certain things by his mom, some different things by his dad, and some very different things by others.

2.) Thus when he is with mom it is one way, when with dad another way, and when with others yet another way.

3.) Therefore an infant believer is tossed to and fro by the various teachers he has just like a baby is influenced by others which hold sway over him in one way or another.

d. And carried about (περιφερόμvoι--to be borne about hither and thither, to be whirled about).

1.) An infant, before he learns to walk, has to be carried about, and he will be taken wherever his bearer takes him.

2.) He will even be taken places he does not want to go, like one of our fine church nurseries!

3.) But he is taken there because he does not have the power to resist.

4.) An infant in the Lord can be controlled by a false teacher, a false preacher, or a false evangelist, especially if he is not availing himself to sound doctrinal teaching.

e. With every wind of doctrine ('ανέμω διδασαλιάς).

1.) Please notice that the one not grounded in the Word is subject to being carried away from God by EVERY WIND OF DOCTRINE!

2.) A wind of doctrine pictures an object's direction being set by the direction and power of the wind which blows against it.

3.) The wind of false doctrine is ever blowing, and its power is proportionate to the yieldingness it finds in us.

4.) There is only one source of doctrine that should ever influence us, its God's Holy Word as it is empowered by His Holy Spirit.

5.) Have you resisted the winds of false doctrine that are blowing against us today? Like: abortion, euthanasia, evolution, atheism, immorality, prosperity theology, the improper usage of the gifts, Christian rock music, etc.

f. By the sleight of men (κυβεία-play at dice).

1.) Every false doctrine is taught by the sleight of men who seek to take advantage of you as they teach falsely:

- A fetus is not a human being, it is just protoplasm so you can do what you want to with it.

- A man can become a god, if he becomes good enough while he is here on earth.

- There is no hell, you only imagine that there is; therefore you have nothing to fear.

- The Bible is the product of man, not God's inspiration of the Holy men who wrote it.

- God is dead, in fact, He never lived so why should you worship and serve Him?

- All things are relative, there are no absolutes; therefore do what you want to do.

- There are many ways to get to heaven, just choose the one you like best.

2.) But each false doctrine denies the truth that is self-evident in the lie, and it calls God a lair!

3.) Every false doctrine can only be promoted by the deception with which the deceiver seeks to deceive those who are being deceived by his devious and deceptive words and deeds.

4.) Oh dear child of God, be perfected in Him and you'll never be deceived by the deceiver!

g. And the cunning craftiness (πανουργία).

1.) This cunning craftiness comes from the Master Deceiver who promotes himself as an angel of light, II Corinthians 11:13, 14. Satan comes to us many times as "further light given," and attempts to deceive us into believing that God is keeping us in the dark, is keeping us from enjoying everything the world offers to us, and is keeping us from experiencing things for ourselves. He wants us to do it so we'll know experientially that it is good or bad. But God wants us to trust Him that it is bad if He says that it is. We do not need to experience it to know that it is bad. It is bad, if God says that it is bad! I hope you realize that this is exactly what Satan did to Eve in the Garden of Eden, Genesis 3:5, *"For God doth know that in the day ye eat thereof, then your eyes shall be opened, and ye shall be as gods, knowing good and evil."*

2.) And all who follow him will seek to do the same to you as quickly as is possible.

3.) You do not have a chance to survive if you remain in the infancy stage of your FAITH!

4.) Grow up in Jesus, be strong in the faith, reach the measure of the stature of the fullness of Christ, Ephesians 4:13c.

h. Whereby they lie in wait to deceive (πρὸσ τὴν μεθοδείαν τῆς πλάνης).

1.) The end view of all the activity of those who deceive is to systematize the error they are promoting.

2.) How successful have they been? Look at the various religions in the world today and you'll find your answer.

3.) Every one is the direct result of the activity of those who seek to carry away those who are infants or have remained infants in the faith.

4.) Where are you in the faith? Will it keep you safe from false doctrine? Will you begin the perfection process, right now?

Now before we continue this lesson I want to refresh your memories as to what we have already learned from this passage. We first looked at the Purpose of the Gifts in verse twelve. Then we looked at the Duration of the Gifts in verse thirteen. Next we began to look at the Necessity of the Gifts in verses fourteen through sixteen, and we want to continue along those lines now. We have already studied verse fourteen so we'll begin our study with verse fifteen.

2. So that we may grow up in the Body of Christ, 15b.

a. But how is this to be accomplished? By speaking the truth in love, 15a.

The word translated speaking means to maintain the truth in its proper prospective so that we can always speak it in love ('αληθεύοντες--nom/pl/masc/part/pres).

1.) The Apostle Paul has already laid out for the Ephesian believers how they can obtain the truth, 4:11.

2.) And if they had submitted themselves unto the preaching-teaching ministries of the evangelists, the pastors, and the teachers, then they would have been grounded in the truth!

3.) But they would not yet be ready for retirement since they must maintain the truths they had been taught in order to retain their battle readiness.

4.) This would be true because everyday of their lives truth would come face-to-face with error.

5.) Therefore they were to maintain truth at full alert status all the days of their lives.

6.) And if truth was not battle ready at all times, then error would overcome truth.

- In WWII we lost several ships and many lives in the battle of Guadalcanal because error overtook truth.

- I am told that our naval intelligence people told our officers that the Japanese would not fight at sea at night because of their poor eyesight.

- Oh, that our officers would have known the truth, maintained the truth, and acted on the truth.

- But how many Christian lives have been lost due to the same type of oversight?

b. We have learned that truth must be held in readiness at all times, but now we learn that it must be held in love!

1.) Of course, the word used for love ('ααπῆ) refers to a self-sacrificing type of love.

2.) But what does it mean?

- It means that we must hold all truth and share all truth with others with the same intent, purpose, and manner as God shared it with us.

- So, when I think about being delivered from the Lake of Fire: my mind, my heart, and my soul are flooded with the love God expressed to me when He delivered me.

- And it means that when I share the Gospel truth of Hell's literal fire with someone else that I'll see him as one who desperately needs to be delivered, just like I was!

- Yes, I deserved to go to Hell, and so does everyone else, but God's truth expressed in love as He gave His Son to die on Calvary's cross, delivered us from the torments of Hell because we had accepted Jesus as our Savior.

- Oh, praise the Lord for speaking the truth in love to us!

c. And what are the results we experience if we grow up in Him in all things?

1.) We become perfected or complete in Christ.

2.) We become equipped to do the work of God.

3.) We strengthen the Body of Christ.

4.) We become united in the Faith.

5.) We obtain knowledge about the Son of God.

6.) We measure up to the fullness of Christ.

7.) We are no longer tossed to and fro by every wind of doctrine.

8.) We speak the truth in love.

9.) We grow up in Him in all things.

- All things pertaining to godliness.

- All things relating to true holiness.

- All things belonging to Scriptural righteousness.

10.) We identify with Our Head, Jesus Christ.

- The Body now functions at the command of Christ whom the Father has appointed to be the Head.

- The Body is unified in its efforts to serve its Head just as God planned it to do because each member of the Body has found his place within the Body and is performing his God given function as unto the Lord.

- The Body is an honor and glory unto its Head, our Lord Jesus Christ.

- The Body fulfills its God given mission under the supervision of its Head, the Son of God.

11.) We work mutually together for the glory of God putting aside every fond ambition.

12.) We become all that God intended for us to be to the praise of His glory both now and forever.

In points one and two we introduced you to the tremendous possibility that we can Grow Up In Him. Now I want to build on that reality as we begin to look deeper into what a proper relationship with Christ will do for any local church as a whole, and what it will do for the individuals that make up any local church: IT WILL BECOME THAT GLORIOUS CHURCH that God desires every non-believer to see, and every believer to become part of as soon as he is saved. Are you ready for some real soul food? Then notice the last benefit of growing up in Him.

3. We work mutually together in the Body of Christ.

   a. Because we are Scripturally united to our Head, Jesus Christ, Ephesians 4:15c.

   1.) The Head controls the Body as a whole, and the individuals as parts who make up the whole.

   2.) The Body willingly submits to its Head because it understands that it cannot Biblically function otherwise.

3.) The Head and the Body thus work together in Glorious Harmony for the cause of Christ here on earth, Ephesians 4:16a.

b. Because we as the Body of Christ are fitly joined together and compacted by that which every joint supplies.

1.) The Body of Christ can only function properly when it works as one united whole under Christ's supervision.

2.) Therefore it must be fitly joined together or joined together perfectly, συναρμολογούμενον.

- This process is accomplished by not being conformed to the image of this world, Romans 12:2, *"And be not conformed to this world."*

- But by being transformed by the renewing of the mind so that we can know the will of God for our lives, Romans 12:2b, *"but be ye transformed by the renewing of your mind, that ye may prove what is that good, and acceptable, and perfect, will of God."* Have you noticed how quickly those who profess to be Christians adopt the ways of the world as it relates to hairstyle, dress, language, and casualness concerning the sacred things of God? What a shame it is that we Christians do not set the style instead of letting the world do it.

3.) And it must be compacted or it must be caused to come together as a united whole.

- The musicians, those who offer prayers, the preacher, and the people must all work together to bring glory to God so that an atmosphere is created where God can be worshiped in Spirit and Truth.

- This is a beautiful thing to see!

- It also is a marvelous thing to experience!

- And it is what God wants us to experience each time we enter into His Holy presence!

4.) Now the fitly joining together, and the compacting together is accomplished as each member of the Body finds his place in the Body of Christ, and then begins to do it as UNTO THE LORD!

- Thus I supply what you lack, and you supply what I lack so that we neither one lack anything.

- And by this process there is added to us an oversupply so that our SUPPLY EXCEEDS OUR NEEDS.

- Why then do we struggle? Why are we so easily defeated?

- Because there are things in our lives which are more important to us than doing the will of God.

c. Because we work effectively in the measure of every part. NO WASTED ENERGY, NO MISGUIDED EFFORTS AT ALL, AND NO SELF-WILL EXPRESSED!

1.) Each member of the Body does what God has called him to with all of his heart AS UNTO THE LORD!

2.) He doesn't try to do what someone else has been called to do because he knows that would be sinful, and do great harm to the Body of Christ.

3.) Thus there is no under-working, nor over-working by any member of the Body.

4.) But each member works in harmony with all the other parts of the Body for the common good of the whole, and then and only then, does the Body experience the effectiveness that God wants it to have. Oh, that would be GLORY for me and you!

d. Because we make increase of the Body unto the edifying of itself in love.

1.) The Body of Christ becomes stronger through this process that benefits it greatly.

2.) The Body of Christ now has realized how godly love for the cause of Christ will overcome all the rough edges of all the parts so that it can "hum" along as it works.

- Each member of the Body should say to God, Lord, GRIND OFF ALL MY ROUGH EDGES so that I can mesh well with all the other parts of the Body.

- I want this done because your work is more important to me than me getting my own willful way.

- In fact, it is more important than any of us, or all of us getting our own ways.

3.) And when this attitude is expressed by all the members of the Body of Christ, the BODY BECOMES SO BEAUTIFUL THAT NO MORTAL BEHOLDING IT CAN BEHOLD ANY UNCOMELINESS IN ANY OF ITS PARTS!

4.) Oh, Dear people of God, this is what God wants the whole world to see when it looks at HIS CHURCH!

5.) And this is what the world will see when this passage is put into practice in any local church.

- Is this what you want for your church?

- Are you willing to let God grind off all your rough edges?

- If you are, God will do the work of the lapidarian so that you become the polished gem He desires you to become.

D. The Responsibility We Have To The Gifts Given To The Church By God.

1. First, we must identify each gift that He has given to the Church, and then determine if it has been given to us personally.

2. Secondly, we must understand the purpose for which the gift was given to us.
3. Thirdly, we must use the gift that God has given to us under the supervision of the Holy Spirit.
4. Fourthly, we must work in consort with all others who have received gifts from God realizing that their gift is just as important as our gifts.
5. Fifthly, we must realize that our rewards will be given according to how well we used the gift given to us by God.
6. Sixthly, we must be content with the gift we have been given because God has given it according to our ability to use it.
7. Seventhly, we must praise God for the gifts He has given unto man, and the Church.
   a. There seems to be different categories of gifts that are given to us.
      1.) The gifts categorized as "what hast thou" start with what we call natural talent, and go on to include anything supernatural, I Corinthians 4:7. The word gift is not used in this verse, but it certainly is implied in what is said.
      2.) The gifts (χάρισμα) categorized as those which can be imparted from one to another, or better, the use of my gift to help you and your need, Romans 1:11.
      3.) The gifts (δόματα) categorized as given by God, Ephesians 4:8.
      4.) The gifts (χαρισμάτων) categorized as given by the Holy Spirit, I Corinthians 12:4-10.
      5.) The gifts (prophecies, tongues, knowledge) categorized as they that fail, they that shall cease, and that which shall vanish away, I Corinthians 13:8. The word gift is not used here, but the three gifts listed here are referred to as gifts in the passage listed above, 4.).

6.) The gifts (categorized as general gifts: helps, governments, ministry, exhortation, giveth, ruleth, mercy, and hospitality), I Corinthians, 12:28; Romans 12:6-8. These are listed as gifts (χαρίσματα) in Romans 12:6.

7.) The gifts categorized as abiding gifts, I Corinthians 13:13. The word gifts is not listed in this verse, but is implied from I Corinthians 12:31.

b. However, every gift given by God should be considered most precious, and should be used with the greatest care and the purest heart.

This will be true when we learn the More Excellent Way that the Apostle Paul tells us about in I Corinthians 12:31. I'm striving with all of my strength to not only find that way, but to excel in that way.

SECTION TWO

Scripture Text:
1 Corinthians 1:7, 3:1-3, 12:12, 14:12

Scripture Text: I Corinthians 1:1-3.

Theme: A More Excellent Way.

Title: The Unscriptural Exercise By A Church Of The Gifts That God Had Given Unto It.

Introduction: Having presented the five classes of individuals God has given to the Church as gifts, and having studied their work within the Church we are now ready to look at the One Church in the New Testament that is given more information about gifts than all the rest of the churches mentioned in the New Testament put together. Thus it is the prime object of our present study. However, we learn more about its misuse of the gifts than we learn about its correct usage of the gifts. Let us therefore listen to the Apostle Paul as he addresses the issue which surfaced in its midst.

He says that they were zealous of spiritual gifts, I Corinthians 14:12, and that they came behind in not one gift, I Corinthians 1:7. This church was a leading, if not the leading church in the exercise of spiritual gifts. That is clearly established in the Bible! In light of this statement I therefore want to know just how spiritual the people were in that church. Once I know how spiritual they were, then I can determine if their ability to exercise all the gifts came from their spirituality or in spite of their lack of true spirituality. Let us then begin our careful study of this church.

I. ITS FALSE STANDARDS SET FORTH.
   A. Our Exercise Of The Gifts Makes Us Superior Christians, I Corinthians 4:6, 7, 18; 5:2, 6.
      1. It has been my experience in the Christian world that those who have power and/or talent need to be very careful to avoid letting these go to their head.
      2. The believers at Corinth let their exercise of the gifts puff them up, and caused them to glory in their abilities instead of glorying in Christ.
      3. This same attitude permeates some who are in the ministry regardless of what stripe they may be.
         a. In their eyes we are not spiritual if we do not exercise the gifts.

- b. In their eyes we are on a much lower spiritual plane than those exercising the gifts.
- c. But in God's eyes some mighty humble and quiet saints stand first in His eyes both now and forever.
- d. It is far, far better to stand first in the eyes of God than among the brethren, or the world.

B. Our Exercise Of The Gifts Puts Us Above Apostolic Authority. Now I Corinthians 4:18-21 says, *"Now some are puffed up, as though I would not come to you. But I will come to you shortly, if the Lord will, and will know, not the speech of them which are puffed, but the power. For the kingdom of God is not in word, but in power. What will ye? Shall I come unto you with a rod, or in love, and the spirit of meekness?"*

1. If this passage were not so pathetic it would cause me to break out in laughter.
2. Do these carnal believers really think that they know more than the Apostle Paul does?
3. How could they so quickly forget who had led them to the Lord, I Corinthians 4:15?
4. But their exercise of the gifts had blinded them to the point that they thought they knew everything.
5. Isn't it strange how so many who are so young in the faith purport to know so much more than those who have walked with Jesus so long and so close?
6. But if you can exercise a gift, then you have the right to set yourself up as an authority on all matters—at least that is what some would like us to believe.

C. Our Exercise Of The Gifts Frees Us From The Standards Set Forth In The Word Of God.

1. We see that the rules of common courtesy were violated, I Corinthians 11:17-21.

2. We see that no self-examination was done before the communion service was observed, I Corinthians 11:27-32.
3. We see that this type of conduct seems to be present in far too many lives of those who are charismatic in practice.
   a. A noted evangelist is absent from the pulpit for about three months when he is found guilty of gross and prolonged immoral conduct, and then it is back to business as usual.
   b. A well-known husband and wife healing team have to go to a medical doctor because neither one of them could heal her "pink eye" although they are in the midst of a healing campaign.
   c. A so-called spiritual giant fashions his own rules so that a family problem can be solved.
   d. A prominent faith healer has a walk-in vault to store her riches in while the poor are destitute all around her.
   e. A faith healer goes to another state to have eye surgery even though he has his own hospital, and is supposed to be able to heal all manner of disease.
4. Their so-called doctrines are nothing, but a set of man-made rules fashioned to suit their own fleshly needs.
5. When your standards are not God's standards they are non-Biblical in nature, unscriptural in content, and unacceptable unto God.

II. ITS FALSE SPIRITUALITY EXAMINED.
   A. They Were Evidently Saved, I Corinthians 1:2, 4, 9, 10, 3:1.
   B. But They Certainly Were Not Spiritual (πνευματικοῖς), I Corinthians 3:1.
   C. And This Was Evidenced By Their Actions:
      1. For we hear the Apostle Paul say to them that they were carnal. Ye are carnal. And, are ye not carnal, 3:1, 3, 4?

a. Galatians 5:19-21 lists the works of the flesh (σαρκός) for us.

b. There are seventeen manifestations of the flesh listed in this passage.

c. Would you believe that you find fourteen of the seventeen listed, and the other three implied in the church at Corinth?

As you will notice on the overview sheet which follows, the Greek words used in Galatians 5:19-21 TO IDENTIFY THE WORKS OF THE FLESH are all found in I and II Corinthians except for the words translated witchcraft (φαρμακεία), murder (φόνοι), and revelling (κῶμοι). Also please remember that the Greek word which appears in the center column is the same Greek word which is found across the page although the translation does vary at times.

However, I think that it is implied in I Corinthians 14:26 that the Corinthians were seeking revelation through unscriptural methods since every time they came together everyone had a revelation. This certainly would be a form of witchcraft. Also their noted rebellion against God's laws would constitute witchcraft according to I Samuel 15:23. Murder by tongue is implied in I Corinthians 10:10. Reveling is pictured in I Corinthians 11:17-21.

Whatever your level of spirituality is I'm sure that you can see that a church having fourteen of the seventeen works of the flesh practiced in it is not a suitable example for a New Testament Church. I therefore ask you to look the chart over, and then ask God how you should react to it. May you be Spirit led as you do it!

SUMMARY OF THE WORKS OF THE FLESH FOUND IN GALATIANS 5:19-21 WHICH ARE ALSO FOUND IN THE CHURCH AT CORINTH.

The Fleshly (σαρκός) Works:
Galatians 5:19-21.

Ye Are Carnal (σαρκικοί):
I Corinthians 3:3.

King James Version	Englishman's Greek N.T.	Corinthian Passages
adultery	adultery μοιχεία	adultery, I Cor. 6:9.
fornication	fornication πορνεία	fornication, I Cor. 5:1, II Cor. 12:21.
uncleanness	uncleanness 'ακαθαρσία	uncleanness, II Cor. 12:21.
lasciviousness	lascentiousness 'ασέλγεια	lasciviousness, II Cor. 12:21
idolatry	idolatry εἰδωλολατρεία	idolatry, I Cor. 6:9, 8:14,
witchcraft	sorcery φαρμακεία	see sec. II, RII, C, 1, c, p42, para. 2 for more details.
hatred	enmites 'έχθραι	hatred, II Cor. 2:7, 8.
variance	strifes 'έρεις	contentions I Cor. 1:ll, 3:3 strife, 12:20 debates.

A More Excellent Way

King James Version	Englishman's Greek N.T.	Corinthian Passages
emulations	jealousies ζῆλοι	envyings, I Cor. 3:3, 12:20.
wrath	indignation θυμοὶ	wrath, II Cor. 12:20.
strife	contentions ’εριθεῖαι	strife, II Cor. 12:20.
seditions	divisions διχοστασίαι	divisions, II Cor. 3:3.
heresies	sects αἱρέσεις	heresies, I Cor. 11:19.
envyings	envying φθόνοι	envyings, I Cor 1:12, 3:4. both show envying.
murders	murders φόνοι	murder by tongue, I Cor. 10:10.
drunkenness	drunkenness μέθαι	drunken, I Cor. 11:21.
revellings	revels κῶμοι	I Cor. 11:17-21 shows this was being done.
and such like	like these ‘όμοια τούτοις	the following lists some * of the *and such like* going on in this "spiritual church".

*backbiting, whispering, swelling, tumults, puffed up, extorting, railings, covetousness, effeminacy, abusers of mankind.

d. Now would you tell me how this so-called high level of spirituality could exist in this church with all these works of the flesh being manifested in this church on this level?

1.) This church evidently had more spiritual problems than all of the rest of the churches put together.

2.) And this was your number one gift using church in those days.

e. No wonder Paul called them carnal (σαρκικοῖς), or fleshly.

2. For they were babes (νηπίοις) in Christ, I Corinthians 3:1.

a. Paul uses the word, babe, to characterize them, it means one not yet speaking, and infant, or one below the age of adulthood.

b. They still needed the milk of the Word, I Corinthians 3:2a.

c. They were not able to handle the MEAT of the Word (βρῶμα), and they had never been able to handle it, I Corinthians 3:2. How many churches would this be true of today?

1) This refers to that which needs to be chewed.

- Would you say that in most churches today that you would hear milk preaching rather than meat preaching?

- Which would you say is needed the most?

2.) It would refer to doctrines and practices going on beyond the basics. How many churches are beyond the basics?

d. And would you believe that these things were true of them even though they had sat under the ministry of the Apostle Paul for eighteen months (Acts 18:11), and had probably had at least three more years to grow after he left (three years at Ephesus before he wrote I Corinthians).

e. They were four and one-half years old in the Lord, but they were still babes.

    f. They were four and one-half years old in the Lord, but they were still, carnal!

3. For they walked as men, I Corinthians 1:10, 11; 3:3 (ʾάνρωπον περιπατεῖτε).

    a. This was evidenced by the divisions (σχίσματα- splits or tears) among them, I Corinthians 1:10.

    b. It was manifested by the contentions (ʾέριδες) among them, I Corinthians 1:11.

    c. It was made clear by the envying (ζῆλος- emulations) among them, I Corinthians 3:3a.

    d. It was known to all by the strife (ʾέρις) among them, I Corinthians 3:3b.

    e. And it was beyond question because of the divisions (διχοστασίαι-standing apart) among them, I Corinthians 3:3c, 1:12.

4. For they were puffed up: to inflate, to puff up, to become vain, or to be arrogant.

    a. In I Corinthians 4:6 Paul exhorts them not to be continually being puffed up by an outside source (φυσιοῦσθε- p/pass/subj), the devil.

    b. In I Corinthians 4:18 he says that they were puffed up at that very moment (ʾεφυσιώθησαν-aor 1/pass) by an outside source, the devil.

    c. And in I Corinthians 5:2 he says that what had been characteristic of them in the past was characteristic of them in the present, and that it would continue so long as they let the devil puff them up (πεφυσιωμένοι-perf/part).

    d. Then in I Corinthians 5:6 he tells them that their glorying is not good (καύχημαι-boast, laudatory, testimony)

5. For they were disrespectful to God's apostle, I Corinthians 4:9, 10, 14 in particular and 1-18 in general.

6. And they were rejecters of God's Holy Word, I Corinthians 4:17.
    a. Is it therefore any wonder that Paul had to admonish them in so many areas, I Corinthians 4:14?
    b. Is it therefore any wonder that they had so many problems?

III. ITS FALSE PRACTICES EXPOSED.
   A. This Is By No Means An Exhaustive List.
      1. We would have to study the whole of both books to list them all.
      2. But it does hit the high points.
   B. This Is Only A Selective List.
      1. They were glorying in men instead of God, I Corinthians 3:21.
      2. They had allowed a fornicator to go undisciplined, I Corinthians 5:1, 4, 5.
      3. They were taking their brothers and sisters to court, I Corinthians 6:1, 5, 6, 7.
      4. They had failed to practice personal and ecclesiastical separation, I Corinthians 5:11, 6:18, 10:16-22.
      5. They were having problems with marriage, divorce, and remarriage, chapter seven.
      6. They did not understand the weaker brother concept, I Corinthians 8:8, 10:28.
      7. They failed to honor the apostleship of Paul, chapter nine.
      8. They didn't recognize the difference between male and female, I Corinthians 11:1-16.
      9. They abused the Lord's Supper, I Corinthians 11:21, 28-31.
      10. They had real problems as to how the gifts were to be used, chapters twelve through fourteen.
      11. They misunderstood the resurrection, chapter fifteen.
      12. They were not inclined to submit to leadership, I Cor. 16:16.

Would you want your church to be like this church? I don't think that any person in his right mind would! But it exercised the gifts more than any other church we know of in the New Testament. Why would this be? Perhaps because at one time this church had been the spiritual church God wanted it to be, and He had bestowed upon it an abundance of gifts. However, as time passed and sin slipped in God took away the gifts; therefore they felt that they had to keep up the good appearance. Thus in this frame of mind they began to pretend to still have the gifts, and began to practice all the activities that are condemned in this church. By doing this, at least in their minds, they were still as spiritual as ever.

Scripture Text: I Corinthians 12:4-11.

Theme: A More Excellent Way.

Title: The Scriptural Evaluation Of The Gifts Given To The Church By God.

Introduction: By now I trust that you have the feel of this series of lessons. We have exhorted you not to be tossed to and fro by every wind of doctrine, and we have introduced the gifts to you so that you know what we are talking about. Thus we are ready to evaluate the gifts in a six-fold manner. This will not be my evaluation—it will be a Scriptural evaluation that I trust will please God. If it is Scriptural, it will please God! My earnest prayer is that the Holy Spirit will lead us in all that is said and done. He who authored the Scriptures certainly can teach us all truth as it pertains to all Scriptural matters. Would you pray with me that we all will accept all that is true in this lesson?

I. ACCORDING TO SCRIPTURAL PRIORITY.

   A. There Is Much Confusion As To Which Gift Is Best.

      1. Some use their so-called ability to speak "in tongues" as the standard by which you can determine whether a person is Spirit filled or not.

         a. But you'll never find a truly Spirit-filled person promoting this false standard.

         b. Nor can you ever find this standard found in the Word of God.

         c. Therefore we should never use it ourselves, nor allow anyone else to superimpose it upon us.

      2. Others will point to their ability to heal the physically ill as their certification of the Spirit's fullness.

         a. As far as I know there has not been ONE VERIFIED case of healing ever presented in behalf of these so-called divine healers.

         b. I do not mean to say that God does not heal—He does heal and many times in marvelous ways.

      c. What I'm saying is that as it pertains to the so-called healers—not one certified healing is on the record, at least that I am aware of as of today.

      d. That causes me to be very skeptical of anything and everything they say and do! And it makes me want to find certified medical records, if they exist, which begin at least two years prior to and up to the supposed healing. Certified medical records as to what was wrong with the person at the moment the healing took place so that I can rest assured that he was healed of what he said he was sick of. And certified medical records after the supposed healing took place (up to five years after) so that everyone will know for sure whether the sickness came back or not.

         I think this would remove all doubt as to whether a true healing took place or not. I really want to know the truth, and I trust that you do also. I would think that every faith healer would be anxious to verify his healings, don't you?

  3. Would it not be much better to simply see what God has to say rather than see what every man has to say?

B. God Has Taken The Time To Show Us What He Thinks.

  1. First of all as it pertains to the charismatic gifts themselves, I Corinthians 12:8-10

      a. Wisdom, knowledge, and faith lead the list, I Corinthians 4:8, 9a.

      b. Then follows healings, miracles, and prophecies, I Corinthians 4:9b, 10a.

      c. And last of all comes: discerning of spirits, speaking in tongues, and interpretation of tongues, I Corinthians 4:10b.

         1.) Healing is in the second group of three.

         2.) And speaking in tongues is in the last group of three. The last group! The very last group!

3.) Does this say anything to you about their importance in the Church, to man, and to God?

4.) Does God's divine order have any significance to you at all?

2. Secondarily, as it pertains to the charismatic gifts in relation to other gifts, I Corinthians 12:28, 29.

   a. Please notice very carefully that God has set the order of priority for the gifts listed here!

   b. Notice that this priority is to be observed by and in the Church.

   c. Now take the time to zero in on God's order:

      1.) An apostle ('αποστόλους) was one who followed Jesus from the baptism of John, who had witnessed the resurrected Lord, and had been selected by Jesus, Act 1:22. Later, one apostle would be selected by the other eleven apostles, and the one hundred twenty disciples who were in the upper room.

      - We do not have any apostles today because none can meet these requirements.

      - Nevertheless in the early church they had the number one ranking. The last apostle, John, died in about 98-100a.d.

      2.) A prophet (προφήτας) was one who spoke or wrote the Word of God because he was moved by the Holy Spirit, II Peter 1:21.

      - We do not have any prophets today because we have all the revelation we need from God.

      - Yet in the early church their position was number two, John fits into this category also.

      3.) A teacher (διδασκάλους) is one who imparts the doctrines and principles found in God's Word to others with the purpose of training them.

- We do have teachers today, they are number three here, but since there are no apostles and prophets today—they become number one!

- If you want to have the best gift today—be a teacher of the Word of God.

- A pastor must be apt to teach, I Timothy 3:2f.

- God gave the pastor and the teacher to the Church, Ephesians 4:11.

4. A miracle worker (δυνάμεις) came next. He was one who did works of power.

- This gift is not available to us today.

- We'll elaborate on this when we present a whole lesson on this subject.

5.) A healer ('αμάτων) took fifth place in God's hierarchy of gifts.

- Healings as performed in the early church through the gift of healing are not for today.

- It was fourth among the charismatic gifts, and it is fifth among all gifts.

- Only God heals in this time frame, the Church Age from the end of the first century on.

6.) Helps ('αντιλήψεις) refer to those who aided, assisted, or helped others.

- Perhaps this refers to any job needing to be done by anyone who was not a leader in any other area of service.

- Would you please notice that God considers helps a greater gift than speaking in tongues?

- Don't ever forget that or let anyone deceive you about this truth!

7.) Next comes governments (κυβερνήσεις) which means to steer or direct such as a pilot or helmsman steers a ship.

- This is a lesser gift in importance than helps, but it is still a greater gift than speaking in tongues.

- Please open your minds and hearts to the facts, then let the Holy Spirit who inspired the Scripture teach you good and sound doctrine.

8.) Speaking in tongues (γένη γλωσσῶν-kinds of tongues), or the ability to speak a language formerly foreign to you or unlearned by you.

- Does the term "dead last" mean anything to you?

- That is where God ranks tongues, DEAD LAST!

- It is higher than nothing else, but it is lower than everything else.

- Any gift that you have is evidently better than speaking in tongues.

II. ACCORDING TO ECCESIASTICAL USAGE.
   A. All Gifts Are Given For The Edification Of The Body, I Corinthians 14:12.
      1. Not one gift was to ever be used to glorify self, nor to gratify the flesh.
      2. Each gift was to be used to help others, never self.
      3. The gift, which ever gift it may be, is given by the Holy Spirit so that you may meet the need of a person that you could not have met without the gift.
      4. And when you have exercised your God given gift it should leave him stronger in the Lord.
   B. The Gifts Are Given So That Each Man May Profit From Their Usage, I Corinthians 12:7, 12-27.

1. Not profit him in particular, but profit the one the gift is exercised upon.
2. Just think that through for a minute.
    a. Healing benefits the one receiving the healing.
    b. Prophecy benefits those receiving it.
    c. Miracles benefit those receiving them.
C. But The Church At Corinth Sought Only The Gifts Which Caused Them To Be Seen Of Men For They Were Carnal, I Corinthians 3:3.
    1. What a tragedy this was for that church!
    2. But little has changed, even today, for few want to exercise the help ministries of the Church while ever so many want to exercise the leadership gifts.

III. ACCORDING TO SPIRITUAL COMMITMENT.
A. The Scripture Clearly States That The Holy Spirit Dispenses Gifts As He Wills, I Corinthians 12:11.
    1. That means that I have nothing to do with it at all! NOTHING TO DO WITH IT AT ALL!
    2. He gave the gift as it was needed to accomplish the will of God in the life of the person receiving it.
    3. That person could not have done the will of God had he not received the gift.
B. The Holy Spirit Dispenses The Gifts To Compensate For Our Weaknesses.
    1. Some people are naturally endowed with special abilities, they have no need of a gift in the area of their ability.
    2. Others are not naturally endowed; therefore they have a need to receive a gift.
    3. The receiving of the gift points up a weakness rather than demonstrating a spiritual strength.

C. These Gifts Therefore Were Not Earned, No One Merited Them, Nor Could Anyone Receive Them Through Prayer Or Practice.
   1. If they could be earned, why are they called gifts?
      a. The word charismatic comes from the word (χαρισμάτων-χάρισμα) meaning a free favor, a free gift, or a free benefit.
      b. How can one earn that which is free?
   2. If they could be merited, then why are they called gifts instead of rewards?
   3. If they could be received through prayer, why does the Scripture tell us that the Holy Spirit dispenses them as He wills?
   4. If they can be obtained through practice, how can they express our spirituality?
   5. And if anyone can learn to do these things, how can they be supernatural endowments of God?

IV. ACCORDING TO ALL-AROUND AVAILABILITY.
   A. All These Gifts Were Not Available To All People, I Corinthians 12:28-30. Let us listen to what the Apostle Paul says to the people at Corinth, *"And God hath set some in the church, first apostles, secondarily prophets, thirdly teachers, after that miracles, then gifts of healings, helps, governments, diversities of tongues. are all apostles? are all teachers? are all workers of miracles? have all the gifts of healing? do all speak with tongues? do all interpret?*
      1. The obvious answer to each question asked in these verses is, NO!
      2. Therefore these gifts were not available even to ALL spiritual people.
      3. Would you let that statement sink into your heart?
   B. Not Everyone Received These Gifts, I Corinthians 12:11.
      1. The Holy Spirit Dispenses Each Gift, And Every Gift AS HE WILLS!

      a. I could beg, plead, cry, and yearn with all my heart, and not receive a single gift unless He willed it.

      b. I could pray, live a devoted life, and sacrifice for my Lord, and not receive a single gift unless He willed it.

  2. And it is a sinful practice to desire that which the Holy Spirit has not willed to give you! It is still a sinful practice today to do it, and it will always be a sinful practice to seek that which is not the will of God for your life.

V. ACCORDING TO HISTORICAL PERMANENCE.

  A. With The Passing Away Of The Apostles These Gifts Passed Away Also.

  B. Thus Gifts Are Not Practiced In The Second Century Church.

  C. The Case The Charismatic Would Try To Make As It Pertains To The Last Times Is Without Merit Or Scriptural Foundation.

    1. We have been in the last days since Pentecost, Acts 2:17, then 16.

    2. Peter said that what the charismatic would say is happening today actually happened when Pentecost came.

    3. Can we call Peter a lair? I think not since he was full of the Holy Spirit, Acts 2:4, 14-18.

"But Peter, standing up with the eleven, lifted up his voice, and said unto them, Ye men of Judaea, and all ye that dwell at Jerusalem, be this know unto you, and hearken to my words:"

"For these are not drunken, as ye suppose, seeing it is but the third hour of the day."

"But this is that which was spoken by the prophet Joel:"

"And it shall come to pass in the last days, saith God, I will pour out of my Spirit upon all flesh: and your sons and daughters shall prophesy, and your young men shall see visions, and your old men shall dream dreams:"

"And on my servants and on my handmaidens I will pour out in those days of my Spirit; and they shall prophesy:"

4. Peter said to those listening to him on the Day of Pentecost that what had just happened in verses four through twelve was the fulfillment of what Joel said would come to pass in the last days.

5. So we have been in the last days since that first Pentecost and will be in the last days until Christ comes again.

VI. ACCORDING TO GOD'S MORE EXCELLENT WAY!
   A. Pursue The Lasting Gifts, I Corinthians 12:31, 13:13.
   B. Seek The Will Of God For Your Life, I John 2:17.
   C. Submit To The Teaching Authority Of The Holy Spirit Of God, John 16:13.
   D. Accept The Authority Of The Word Of God, John 12:48.
   E. As Great And Wonderful As The Gifts Were For Their Day They Can't Even Begin To Compare With What We Have Through A Right Relationship With Jesus Christ For He Is Our "UNSPEAKABLE GIFT."

Scripture Text: I Corinthians 12:4-11.

Theme: A More Excellent Way.

Title: The Fleshly Pursuit Of The Gifts Given To The Church By God.

Introduction: We have covered much ground already in our study of the charismatic gifts as we have introduced you to them, and as we have evaluated them. The bottom line as it pertains to what we have studied thus far is this: we have so much more offered to us by God apart from these charismatic gifts that it would be a waste of time to seek them even if they were available to us today. With this great truth flooding our hearts I now want to examine how the gifts were obtained. Now if these are gifts (χαισμάτων), and the Scriptures calls them gifts, then they would come to us without cost or debt. But the Scripture takes it one step beyond this obvious fact, and clearly states that the Holy Spirit divides the gifts to every man severally as HE WILLS. These gifts were obtained ONLY when the Holy Spirit willed to give them. And HE gave them to whomsoever HE WILLED!

I. THREE MISCONCEPTIONS ABOUT OBTAINING THE GIFTS.

   A. That The Gifts Come To The Spiritual Man.

      1. Because he had merited them through his performance of righteous acts that pleased God, thus God rewarded him with these gifts.

         a. Gifts are not merited otherwise they would not be gifts. Just think of your salvation, Romans 6:23, Ephesians 2:8-10, and then ask yourself what you had to do to receive the gift of salvation. You can do nothing to receive a divine gift for the Holy Spirit gives it as He wills. You can only accept what He gives!

         b. Rewards are given for jobs well done, but gifts are given freely—that's why they are called gifts.

      2. Because he had curried the favor of God by his continued praise of God, and through his efforts in behalf of God.

         a. Is God so cheap that His favor could be curried by man? Man's greatest effort could not earn him an audience with God much less a gift from God.

        b. If this were true then the more talented people would have a better chance of receiving these gifts.

        c. But God rewards us according to ability used, not favor curried.

        d. Still this would be reward, not a gift.

    3. Because he had been exalted high enough to receive them in that his spirituality had exceeded many his equal.

        a. Nowhere is this taught in Scripture.

        b. The Holy Spirit gave the charismatic gifts as He willed.

B. That The Gifts Can Be Secured Through Prayer Promises:

    1. Such as John 15:16, *"whatever ye shall ask of the Father in my name, he may give it you."*

        a. This promise pertains in particular to fruit bearing.

        b. It is not a blank check giving us the right to ask for anything we desire.

        c. The gifts were not given in response to prayer, but given only as the Holy Spirit willed.

    2. Such as Matthew 18:19, *"that if two of you shall agree on earth as touching any thing that they shall ask, it shall be done for them by my Father, who is in heaven."*

        a. This promise would need to be utilized in light of this qualifying statement, ask anything that is according to my will.

        b. It is not the will of God that the gifts be given in answer to prayer—they are given as the Holy Spirit wills!

    3. Such as John 15:7, *"ye shall ask what ye will, and it shall be done unto you."*

        a. Doesn't this verse give the charismatic the right to ask for the gifts?

        b. No, the gifts were given only as the Holy Spirit willed—this pattern was never altered anywhere in Scripture.

c. And besides that, the promise is to those who abide in Jesus, and have His Word abiding in them.
      1.) How could anyone meet these two requirements, and still ask for that which would violate the two requirements for asking?
      2.) He couldn't, thus this so-called promise is out for all who pray for the gifts.
C. That The Gifts Can Be Acquired Through Practice.
   1. This is especially true of speaking in tongues when those learning to speak in tongues are told to just let your tongue wag aimlessly.
   2. How can those who speak in tongues teach you to speak in tongues when the Bible says that the gift comes only as the Holy Spirit wills?
   3. How utterly ridiculous this practice is.
   4. A person would have to become a complete fool to be deceived by this utter nonsense.
   5. And for the teacher to say that he had been led by the Holy Spirit to do it borders on blasphemy, if it is not outright blasphemy.
   6. How could you ever learn what only the Holy Spirit is capable of giving to you?
   7. Beware of attributing to the Holy Spirit what has come from another source.

II. SIX FLESHLY REASON FOR TRYING TO OBTAIN THE GIFTS, ye are carnal, I Corinthians 3:1, 3, 4.

A. So That I Can Openly Display My Spirituality.
   1. There is such a fleshly desire to have everyone recognize us as spiritual superstars these days that many will go to any extreme to accomplish this goal.

2. Just being an everyday Spirit-filled, Bible believing, Church going, Christ loving person is not enough.
3. I want to be a giant, and I intend to become one is the philosophy of far too many people these days.
4. The true saint of God is content to be what God would have him to be, and therefore he seeks for nothing else.
5. True spirituality can always be seen when it is lived—it therefore needs no gift to display it.

B. So That I May Boldly Boast Of My Spirituality.
1. Listen to me, I was raised in a church that did this.
2. I've heard people give testimony that they hadn't sinned in six months.
3. Everyone there knew them well enough to know they were lying, but they'd stand up and do the same thing. And no one would call anyone else's hand lest he be exposed by the one he was accusing.
4. He that has to boast about his spirituality has no spirituality to boast about!
5. If I have to tell you that I have it, I don't have it.

C. So That I May Rapidly Advance In My Spirituality.
1. I am not willing to let God advance me at His speed, I want to advance at my own pace is a sure path to failure.
2. Therefore if I display some or all of the gifts, who are you, what is the church, and how can the Bible say that I am not spiritual? Don't you know that I am an absolute authority myself?
3. Being able to use the gifts to put me on top where I want to be is not where God wants me to be.

D. So That I Can Indiscreetly Play Down Your Spirituality.
1. For if I can speak in tongues and you can't, doesn't that mean that you are inferior to me, spiritually?

2. If I can perform miracles, and you can't, doesn't that tell you something about your spirituality?

3. And if I can heal people and you can't, well do I need to say anything else about your spirituality?

E. So That I Can Consciously Overlook My Lack Of True Spirituality.

1. You say that this is not possible.

2. Listen to me, I have had people look me straight in the eye, and say that they had no sin in their lives when their lives were full of sin.

3. The church at Corinth was full of sin, and yet they were a church that exercised the gifts, or claimed to do it.

F. So That I Can Short-circuit The Way To True Spirituality.

1. True spirituality always comes by the way of the cross, not through gift usage.

2. True spirituality humbles the person to the point that he sees only Christ, he seeks only God's will for his life, and he abhors self.

3. What a contrast this is to the pompous dudes who strut before their gullible followers while boasting of the glorious and marvelous deeds they have done for God.

III. FOUR EMPHATIC STATEMENTS ABOUT OBTAINING THE GIFTS.

A. There Are Diversities Of Gifts, I Corinthians 12:4a.

1. There are nine charismatic gifts (χαρισμάτων) listed in Scripture, I Corinthians 12:4-11.

2. There are five types of individuals listed as gifts (καί αὐτὸς 'ἔδωκεν) in the Bible: Ephesians 4:11.

3. There are eight classifications for the gifts listed in the Word ('ἔθετο 'ο θεὸς 'εν τῇ 'εκκλησία), I Corinthians 12:28.

    4. There are seven exhortations added to the seven gifts listed in Romans 12:6 (χαρίσματα κατὰ τὴν χάριν).
    5. And there are three abiding gifts listed in I Corinthians 13:13.
B. All These Gifts Come From God And/Or The Holy Spirit:
    1. I Corinthians 12:4b, but the same Spirit.
    2. Ephesians 4:11, and He, God, gave some.
    3. I Corinthians 12:28, and God hath set.
    4. Romans 12:6, gifts differing according to the grace that is given by God.
    5. I Corinthians 13:13, these abiding gifts are what Paul is talking about when he tells us of A More Excellent Way.
C. The Holy Spirit Dispenses These Gifts As He Wills To Whom He Wills (καθὼς βούλεται), I Corinthians 12:11.
    1. Did you hear what God said in this Passage?
    2. The gifts come to us only as the Holy Spirit wills.
    3. It is His will which determines who gets what gift and when—NOT OUR WILL!
D. These Gifts Were Given According To Our Need As Observed By The Holy Spirit (διαιροῦν ’ιδία ’εκάστω).
    1. No gift was given unless it was absolutely necessary as it pertained to God's redemptive plan.
    2. Christ would not perform a miracle just to do a miracle, neither will the Holy Spirit give a gift without a definite purpose stemming from a particular need.
    3. God is not in the entertainment business—He is in the soul-winning business, and the soul mending business.
E. And these gifts can never be obtained through human efforts.
    1. We cannot through fervent and continual prayer receive any of these gifts.

2. We cannot through sincere and earnest practice master any of these gifts.

3. We cannot through virtuous and pious living earn any of these gifts.

4. We cannot through dedicated and painful privation merit any of these gifts.

5. We cannot through generous and gracious giving to God and man secure any of these gifts.

6. We cannot through meritorious and exemplary service claim any of these gifts.

7. We cannot through earnest and honest seeking find any of these gifts.

F. In light of what we have learned through this lesson do you still feel that it would profit you to seek any one of the so-called charismatic gifts? It is Scriptural to seek God's will, but it is wrong to seek that which is not His will. God's will is for us to seek the More Excellent Way that He has pointed out unto us. It will help us use the gifts that God gives to us the way He intended them to be used.

SECTION THREE

Scripture Text:
1 Corinthians 12:4-10

Theme: A More Excellent Way.

Title: The Nine Charismatic Gifts Introduced By The Apostle Paul.

Introduction: We have just finished focusing our attention upon the church that excelled in the usage of the gifts given to the Church by God. Now before we introduce you to the gifts in particular I want you to listen with me to the Apostle Paul as he tells us why he is writing this portion of God's Word. He does not want us to be ignorant about the spirituals, he wants to identify the source of the gifts, and he wants to set forth the nine charismatic gifts listed in this portion of God's Word. Let's listen to Him!

I. PAUL DOES NOT WANT THE BRETHREN TO BE IGNORANT.

   A. Therefore He Addresses The Brethren ('αδελφοί).

      1. This refers to all those who are believers in Christ.

      2. Since the gifts were given by God to the Church to use for His honor and glory, then every brother needs to know how, when, and where to use any gift.

      3. In other words, know how to use a gift, or do not use it for it would be far better never use a gift than to use it wrongly.

   B. And He Is Doing It So They Will Not Be Ignorant ('αγνοεῖν).

      1. To be ignorant means to be without knowledge.

      2. If we are without knowledge as it relates to how a gift is to be used, then we will not be having the Holy Spirit's help.

      3. Please let Paul inform you as how to properly use any gift.

   C. Thus He Talks To Them About Spirituals (πνευματικῶν).

      1. Spirituals, I Corinthians 12:1, refer to spiritual things in general.

      2. Thus Paul is going to discuss many things under the heading of that which is of a spiritual nature.

      3. Therefore he does talk about spiritual gifts, their source, and how they are to be used to promote unity within the Body of Christ.

4. However in verse four Paul begins to tell us about diversities of gifts (διαιρέσει χαρισμάτων).
   5. And that diversity is readily seen as he names them for us to observe, and study.
   6. This discussion seems to continue on through chapter fourteen.

II. PAUL CAREFULLY IDENTIFIES THE SOURCE OF EACH ONE, I Corinthians 12:11.
   A. Quoting The Greek Text First, And Then Its Translation From The Englishman's Greek New Testament.
      1. The Greek Text Presented: "πάντα δὲ ταῦτα 'ενεργεῖ τὸ 'ἐν καὶ τὸ αὐτὸ πνεῦμα ιαιροῦν 'ιδία 'εκάστῳ καθὼς οὐλεται."
      2. The Greek Text Translated Into English: "all but these things operates the one and the same Spirit dividing separately to each according as He wills."
   B. Studying Its Individual Parts, And Commenting On Each.
      1. But all these things: the nine charismatic gifts.
      2. Operates the one and the same Spirit: the Holy Spirit.
      3. Dividing: giving to this one and not to that one.
      4. Separately: giving the particular gift that is needed to the exact person who is in need of it.
      5. To each: each particular person, not just any person.
      6. According as He wills: as the Holy Spirit determines who gets what, where, when, and for how long.

III. PAUL LISTS EACH GIFT FOR US TO STUDY.
   A. The List: the word of wisdom, the word of knowledge, faith, gifts of healing, the working of miracles, prophecy, discerning of spirits, divers kinds of tongues, and the interpretation of tongues.

B. The Prayer: Lord, I ask in the name of Jesus that YOU will give us all that we need to understand as much as we need so we can use any gift the Holy Spirit gives to us under His supervision for our heart's desire is to seek that More Excellent Way You have set before us.

C. It seems to me that these nine charismatic gifts are unique among the gifts, in that, they are given by the Holy Spirit as He sees fit, when He sees fit, as often as He see fit, so long as He sees fit, and to whomsoever He sees fit. They also seem to be apart from those gifts we call God given natural talent that we read about in I Corinthians 12:28c, Romans 12:6-8, and I Peter 4:8-ll.

Scripture Text: I Corinthians 12:4-11.

Theme: A More Excellent Way.

Title: The Nine So-called Charismatic Gifts Given To Man By God.

Introduction: Now that Paul has finished his introduction to these gifts let us begin to teach you the error of a doctrine which has blown many churches off-course, it has destroyed far too many Christians, and it has shipwrecked some formerly stanch believers in our Lord Jesus Christ—it is the misuse of the gifts given to man by God. Now it is true that many believers have been motivated to serve better, longer, and with their financial resources as never before. But it is not for certain whom they serve: God, man, self, or the devil. Thus a series of messages is needed to set forth what the Bible has to say on this subject. We begin by studying wisdom, knowledge, and faith.

I. WISDOM (σοφίας) prudence, enlightenment.

    A. The Gift Of Wisdom Was Given To The Early Church So That Wise Choices Would Be Made In A Redemptive Context In Light Of The Limited Biblical Knowledge It Had.

        1. Great wisdom was needed to apply the Old Testament and limited New Testament passages to the life situations the early Church faced.

        2. Great wisdom was needed to expound the mysteries of the Word to an unlearned people.

        3. Great wisdom was needed to face the pressures from the Jewish community, the Roman government, and the pagan world the believer found himself in at that time

        4. Great wisdom was needed to set forth the doctrines of the Church as they were being penned by the Scripture writers.

    B. Thus The Gift Of Wisdom Was Given Until The Scriptures Could Be Placed In The Hands Of The Believers So That They Could Avail Themselves To The Wisdom Of God Contained Therein.

        1. Now, if any man lacks wisdom all he has to do is ask God, James 1:5.

            a. He does not have to depend upon the Gift.
            b. All he has to do is avail himself to the promised provision, or to search out the answer in the Word.
        2. This promised provision pertains to the trials one has in living the Christian life.
        3. While the gift of wisdom was given to those who had not full revelation, the promised provision is given to those who work in light of full revelation.
        4. The gift of wisdom worked in anticipation of full revelation, but the promise of wisdom works in light of full revelation.
        5. Oh, how much greater is the promised provision than the gift of wisdom.
    C. The Gift Of Wisdom Was Given Only To Certain Individuals, But The Promise of Wisdom May Be Claimed By Any Believer.
    D. The Gift Of Wisdom Can Be Ask For By ANYONE, ANYWHERE, AND ANYTIME, James 1:5.
        1. If any man—believers for all spiritual matters, but salvation for the lost.
        2. Lacks wisdom—doesn't know how to use the knowledge he has available to him.
        3. Let him ask of God—ask only of God as your final authority.
        4. Who giveth to all men liberally—gives adequately regardless of race, creed, or color.
        5. And upbraideth not—God will not reprove sharply the person for his lack of wisdom.
        6. And it shall be given unto him—God will give him the wisdom he needs to make the proper decision.
    E. Three questions which need to be pondered deeply:
        1. What area of wisdom in particular do you need that is not furnished for you in the Bible?

2. If the gift of wisdom was given to the Church, is its scope limited to Church related matters?

3. If God gives liberally to those who ask, why would anyone need the gift of wisdom?

F. The Gift Of Wisdom Was Temporary, But The Promised Provision Is Permanent.

1. Why then would anyone ever seek that which is inferior (only in the sense that it was superceded by the provision)?

2. He would only do it if he were being tossed to and fro by every wind of doctrine.

3. The truly Spirit led believer seeks the wisdom of God that is provided by the promise of God!

II. KNOWLEDGE (γνώσεως) to know, to perceive, to understand.

A. The Gift Of Knowledge Was The Ability Of The Believer To Retain Knowledge About The Word So That He Could Share It With Others.

B. The Purpose Was To Impart Redemptive Knowledge To Searching Mankind.

1. Man has a knowledge of right and wrong in his heart, Romans 2:14, 15.

2. But he has to have special revelation to know how to be saved, and discern many spiritual matters

3. Before the canon was closed he did not have all that God wanted him to have, thus the gift of knowledge allowed some to proclaim these truths until its need ceased.

C. As Revelation Progressed There Was Less And Less Need For This Gift.

1. All the knowledge that would ever be needed by man to face all the problems of life spiritually would be recorded in God's Holy Word.

2. And this inspired Word of God would be retained through its INSCRIPTURATION.
   a. I do not need any gift of knowledge to know about God—I have the Word of God!
   b. I do not need any more knowledge from God—I have all that I shall ever need in the Bible!
   c. What I need to do is live according to the knowledge I have!
   d. If God were to give me, right now, the gift of knowledge I would not receive one more piece of information about Him than I already have in my Bible! I have His commandments, His concepts, His examples, His laws, His ordinances, His precepts, His statutes, and His testimonies. What more do I need?

D. Eventually The Gift Vanished Away, I Corinthians 13:8b.
   1. Why should I, a child of God, seek after something that has vanished away (καταργηθήσεται-future passive)?
   2. I shouldn't and I won't: for it would be foolish, it would be against the will of God, and it would be an insult to the Lord who gave me His Completed Word.

E. Any Knowledge That I Need From God Can Be Found In His Word; Therefore I Do Not Need To Wait Upon The Holy Spirit To Give Me The Gift.

F. Four Very Sincere Questions?
   1. What piece of knowledge do you need that isn't furnished for you in the Bible?
   2. If the gift of knowledge is Church related, is it relegated to only Church matters?
   3. How thoroughly have you sought for the knowledge you need in the Word of God?
   4. Have you asked those who really know the Bible if they would help you locate the needed information you seek?

5. I have people all the time saying to me, I did not know that was in the Bible!

III. FAITH (πίστις).

A. The Gift Of Faith Was Given To Those Needing To Believe Or Do The Work Of God In A Time Period When They Had Not The Full Bible To Rely Upon.

1. What kind of faith would you have if you had not the complete Bible?

2. How good would your theology be if you had not the whole Word of God?

3. How Biblical would your practices be if you had not full revelation?

4. You see, dear people, they needed the gift of faith, and the Holy Spirit gave it until He completed the Bible.

B. But Their Faith Which Was Gift Faith Cannot Be Compared With Our Measure Of Faith, Romans 12:3.

1. Every man has been dealt a measure of faith.

2. Only those receiving the gift of faith could excel in faith in those days of the early Church.

3. But my measure of faith can be developed into a full faith as I put into practice what I learn from the Word.

C. The Gift Of Faith Was Dependent Upon The Holy Spirit Dispensing It Unto Those Who Needed It While Present Faith Depends Upon The Hearing Of The Word, Romans 10:17, *"So then faith cometh by hearing, and hearing by the word of God."*

1. Why would anyone want the gift of faith these days when he could have full faith as it pertains to all that is found in the Bible by simply hearing God's Word?

       a. The problem does not rest in a lack of information about the faith that God has not given to us, but with us, in that, we have not even begun to study and understand the information about faith that God has given to us.

       b. If most people would spend as much time and effort on understanding WHAT WE DO HAVE as they do in seeking What We Do Not Have they would find themselves so full of faith that they would have no need of gift faith at all.

2. Why would anyone seek after that which only the Holy Spirit gave to a few when he could have that which is available to every believer?

3. Why would anyone seek that which was temporary when he could have that which is permanent?

4. Why would anyone seek after that which he was not sure he would receive when he could have for certain that which God has provided for every believer?

5. Why would anyone seek after the gift of faith not knowing how much faith it would bring to him when he has unlimited faith offered to him by just hearing the Word?

6. Why would anyone do any of these things? Because he has not availed himself to the faith that is available to him in the Bible!

       a. Of course he would have to read the Bible, and then put into practice what he had read to have real faith!

       b. And it would be so much easier just to receive the gift. At least that is what far too many people think!

D. Three Questions You Need To Answer Honestly:

1. What area of your faith isn't covered in the Bible?

2. If the gift of faith is Church related can you have Biblical faith if the area of your doubt is outside Church matters?

3. If faith now comes by hearing the Word can you find fault with God if your faith isn't want you think it should be?

E. Gift Faith Ceased When Full Faith Could Be Obtained By Simply Hearing The Word.
 1. True faith reads the Word, believes the Word, and lives out the Word.
 2. Any method of seeking Biblical faith apart from this simple procedure is destined to fail the seeker, to disappoint the seeker, and ultimately to cause the seeker to become a doubter.
 3. All those who seek that which is outside the will of God are seeking information from the devil.
 4. Don't you ever be guilty of that!

Scripture Text: I Corinthians 12:4-11.

Theme: A More Excellent Way.

Title: Divine Healing Studied, Divine Healing Introduced, IV-a.

Introduction: In the preceding material we introduced you to three of the charismatic gifts: wisdom, knowledge, and faith. At that time we went into some detail relating to these three. Now we turn to the next six charismatic gifts: healing, miracles, prophecy, discerning of spirits, speaking in tongues, and interpreting tongues. I will spend only a little time introducing and studying some of these gifts, but will spend much time on others. Thus we begin with a long introduction to divine healing.

I believe that all healing comes from God, but I also believe that healing may come in a variety of ways—but all from, through, or by God. I believe that all of these various ways may be listed under, four heading:

1. The Lord has so designed the body that it can heal itself through its natural defense systems.
2. The Lord can use medicine or therapy whenever He so desires.
3. The Lord can use surgery when it becomes necessary, humanly speaking and divinely willed.
4. The Lord may use divine intervention where He steps in and heals according to His will.

Whatever method God chooses to use should be praised by all who are related to the healing.

I will also pursue every Biblical means of being healed, and seeing that others are healed, but I will not ever deceive a single person into believing in my ability to heal, in and of myself.

Neither have I or will I ever take a single penny for praying in behalf of the sick person whom God has raised up from a bed of affliction even though I've seen multitudes raised up.

Even when there was gift healing no money should have ever been received for it was God who did the healing, if any healing was done.

I do not believe in faith healers, but I do believe in divine healing. I say this because as a young person I had an attack of acute appendicitis, was on a gurney on the way to the operating room in the Gibson General Hospital in Princeton, Indiana with a high fever, a severe pain in my right side, and an extremely high white cell blood count when God answered the prayers of those who were praying for me.

On the way to surgery a nurse who accompanied me put her hand on my head, and found it cool and normal. She told the doctor who ordered another white cell blood count. He was amazed to find out it was normal also. No one wanted to believe it, so they immediately checked and rechecked everything. All was normal for even the pain in my side was gone. I sure was a happy boy until the doctor said that he would be giving me a shot every three hours for the next twenty-four hours just to make sure that I was truly healed.

I have never had any other trouble with my appendix. I wholly praised God, and those godly people who prayed for me. No oil was poured on me, not a hand was laid on me, and no special words were spoken over me. God healed me in answer to the prayers that were offered up to Him in my behalf.

The practice given below has been followed by me throughout my ministry when I am praying for those who are sick.

1. I tell the sick person the three reasons sickness comes.

The three reasons are explained in the Section 3, IV-c of the Divine Healing study, Roman I of that study, and the A-C sections of that study, pages 82, 83.

2. I ask the sick person to pray unto God until he discerns which of the three reasons applies to him.
3. If confession if needed, then confession must be made.
4. I then read an appropriate portion of Scripture to him.
5. I pray for the sick person according to the will of God.
6. Example: My Father in heaven, I ask in Jesus' name that this person receive all the healing that is according to Your good and holy will for his life at this moment and the hours that follow.

7. How could God not answer that prayer? He would not only hear it, He would answer it according to His will!

8. But perhaps you may ask me what I know about prayer for the sick when it is all on the line.

I know that my wife had laparoscopic colon surgery to remove as small polyp that had been biopsied as benign. The surgery went well for three days, then she began to worsen, and one week later she had to have conventional surgery because she had a "leaker", she had become septic, and she had to have another six inches of her colon removed immediately. It was benign also.

She was in the intensive care unit for seventeen days under heavy sedation. On the eighteenth day at 2:30 in the morning they came in and said that they were going to give her a shot of lasix, and if her kidneys do not start up immediately, then they had done all that they could do.

I prayed and told God the desire of my heart, but prayed a prayer similar to the model I gave you in the preceding material. Now in this situation that prayer took on great significance! I was putting it all in God's hands even though my total being was crying out, God, PLEASE HEAL HER! And He did for in five days she was home!

I also know about sickness and how important it is to pray the effectual fervent prayer of a righteous man. Let me relate one other circumstance that put me to the test so that you can know that I know what it feels like to be totally dependent on God.

I had invasive eye surgery through the Barnes Jewish Hospital in St. Louis on a Sunday and Monday in the late Fall of 2006. The following Sunday and Monday we were in Springfield, Illinois at the University of Southern Illinois Clinic so my wife could be examined in relation to a basal cell carcinoma. The following Monday and Tuesday we were at the University of Iowa Hospital so my wife could have a check up for her Lichen Planus problems. Then the next Monday we were back in Springfield for Mohs surgery for my wife. She came home with thirty-two stitches. And the next Monday we had to be back for her post surgery check up. God was faithful, God is faithful, and God will always be faithful. He answered every prayer during this time of testing to His honor and glory! Praise His Holy and Righteous name. Just about one year later my wife had four-bypass heart surgery. She is home now, and doing well. For this I praise the LORD over and over again!

I. HEALING, ITS MEANING: ('αματῶν) to heal, or to cure the physically ill.

   A. This Is That Divine Ability To Heal A Person Who Is Physically Ill.

      1. The person had to be physically ill to fit into this category.
      2. The healer had the ability to heal those who were physically ill through divine help.
      3. The person cured was make whole from that moment, and did not have a relapse later, nor did the illness return later on due to his lack of faith.
      4. The healer was the instrument God used to heal in a definite and real manner.
         a. He seems to be indispensable to the healing process in those days.
         b. Without him those healed would have not been healed, humanly speaking.

   B. But It Never Depended Upon Human Ability Alone.

II. HEALING, ITS PURPOSE: to authenticate the preached Word, and the preacher.

   A. Notice The Example Of Jesus, Mark 2:9, 10.
   B. Notice The Example Of Peter, Acts 3:11.
   C. Notice The Example Of Philip, Acts 8:6, 7.
   D. Notice The Example Of Paul, Acts 14:8-11.

III. HEALING, ITS DURATION: it lasted until the Word had been authenticated.

    A. God Stills Heals, But Not Through The Healer.

    B. He Heals Through Divine Intervention Apart From The Divine Healer.

    C. Intercessory Prayer Plays A Very Important Part In The Process Today.

        1. Then it seems to have been prayer to God by the healer, answered prayer by God through the healer to the one being healed.

        2. Today it is prayer to God in behalf of the sick one whom God heals through answered prayer, but not through a healer.

    D. Once The Messenger And The Message Had Been Authenticated Divine Healing Stopped As It Relates To The Charismatic Gift.

        1. Therefore I do not seek it—I seek the will of God for my life.

        2. Seeking the will of God is far more important than seeking my heart's desire!

        3. Do we really love God enough to seek His will above our own will even when it may go against our own will? Isn't that the way Jesus Prayed, Luke 22:42?

Scripture Text: I Corinthians 12:9.

Theme: A More Excellent Way.

Title: Divine Healing Studied, The Elements Considered, IV-b.

Introduction: If the modern day faith healers can do the work they say they can then I want to see it done without any staging whatsoever. However, the more I study the subject of divine healing the less apt I am to believe anything associated with the faith healing ministry of today. I therefore want to very carefully look into the Word of God to see what kind of divine healings took place in the Gospels and early Church eras. Then I can know for certain what I have a right to expect from our modern day faith healers. If they are men of God they should be able to do at least as much as the early Church believers did, and all of what they CLAIM they can do. If they can't, then they have no right to call themselves, faith healers!

I. THE FAITH ELEMENT EXPLAINED.

   A. Cures, Where Faith Was Not Evidenced By The Healed.

      1. The man with the withered hand of Matthew 12:9-13.

      2. The demon possessed man of Capernaum, Mark 1:23-28.

      3. The widow's son at Nain, Luke 7:11-15.

      4. The bowed over woman of Luke 13:10-13.

      5. The man with dropsy, Luke 14:1-6.

      6. The servant's ear, Luke 22:50, 51.

   B. Cures, Where Faith Was Evidenced By The Healed.

      1. The woman with an issue of blood, Matthew 9:22; Mark 5:34; Luke 8:48.

      2. Blind Bartimaus, Mark 10:52.

      3. The ten lepers of Luke 17:19.

      4. The blind man at Jericho, Luke 18:42.

      5. The two blind men of Matthew 9:29.

- C. Cures, Where A Third Party's Faith Was Involved In The Healing Process.
    1. Those who brought the palsied man, Mark 2:5.
    2. The centurion in behalf of his servant, Matthew 8:8, 10.
    3. The Syrophenician woman in behalf of her daughter, Matthew 15:28.
    4. The elders in behalf of the sick one, James 5:14-16.
- D. Conclusions Drawn From The Texts Studied.
    1. The faith of the healed does not always determine whether he will be healed or not.
    2. The faith of others can bring about the healing of the sick one whether he has faith or not.
    3. The faith of the healer is always the key issue in any healing taking place.
    4. The healer can never blame those he attempts to heal if healing does not take place, Mark 9:24-29.
    5. Any man or woman blaming the sick one for not being healed is a deceiver.
    6. The divine healer is always at fault when healing does not take place, if he has attempted to heal, but could NOT HEAL!

II. THE HEALING ELEMENT EXPLORED.

- A. What Should I See If Divine Healers Have The Power They Say They Have?
    1. I have the right to demand that they be able to perform all the various types of healings that are presented in the Word of God.
    2. I have a right expect greater miracles than those performed in the Bible if their interpretation of the Word is true.

3. I have the right to ask them to document and authenticate their work so that it is beyond question the work of God. This was done in the Bible, John 9:8-33.

4. The Bible says that I am to test every spirit so that I can determine where it is from: God or the devil, I John 4:1.

5. I would be derelict in duty if I failed to honestly and sincerely make sure of the facts.

B. What Kinds Of Healings Were Performed In The Bible?

1. The dead were brought back to life, Luke 7:22.

   a. The young man of Nain, Luke 7:11-15.
   b. Lazarus, John 11:43, 44.
   c. Dorcus, Acts 9:36, 40.
   d. Eutychus, Acts 20:7, 9, 10.

I WANT TO SEE THIS HAPPEN BEFORE I BELIEVE!

2. The blind were made to see, Luke 7:22.

   a. The two blind men, Matthew 9:27-30.
   b. A blind man, Mark 8:22-26.
   c. Blind Bartimaeus, Mark 10:46-52.
   d. The blind man of John 9:1-7.

I WANT TO SEE THIS HAPPEN BEFORE I BELIEVE!

3. The lame were made to walk, Luke 7:22.

   a. The lame came to him in the temple, Matthew 21:14.
   b. The man born lame was healed, Acts 3:2-7.

I WANT TO SEE THIS HAPPEN BEFORE I BELIEVE!

4. The deaf were made to hear, Luke 7:22.

   a. The deaf man who also had an impediment of speech, Mark 7:32-35.
   b. The deaf son in Mark 9:25.

I WANT TO SEE THIS HAPPEN BEFORE I BELIEVE!

5. The dumb were made to speak, Matthew 15:30.
   a. Dumb possessed by a demon, Matthew 9:32, 33.
   b. Dumb spirit of Mark 9:17, 25.
   c. The dumb spake, Luke 11:14.

I WANT TO SEE THIS HAPPEN BEFORE I BELIEVE!

6. The maimed were made to be whole, Matthew 15:31.

I WANT TO SEE THIS HAPPEN BEFORE I BELIEVE!

7. The sick were made to be well, Matthew 8:16, 9:35.
   a. The leper of Matthew 8:3.
   b. The woman with the issue of blood, Matthew 9:22.
   c. The palsied man of Mark 2:5.
   d. The man with dropsy, Luke 14:1-4.

I WANT TO SEE THIS HAPPEN BEFORE I BELIEVE!

C. What Kind Of Healings Are Being Performed Today?

1. Divine healing by Almighty God with no human instrument being used whatsoever except those who pray.
   a. My prayer to God in your behalf whereby God heals you directly.
   b. Your prayer unto God whereby He heals you directly.
2. Some psychosomatic illnesses are being "cured" by faith healers, but since the cause is not dealt with at the time of the so-called healing new symptoms will appear once again.
   a. Some feel that this type of deception is not harmful since it helps, at least, for a while.
   b. Others know that any deception is destructive at any time, some time for all time.
   c. Knowing God and believing God gives a more lasting cure, and assures me of the ultimate cure.

3. Very little, if any, healing is really happening through charismatic efforts.

   a. If any healing occurs, it occurs directly through God, never through the divine healer.

   b. God heals some in spite of the non-Scriptural practices of those who claim to be godly.

III. THE SUCCESS/FAILURE ELEMENT EXAMINED.

   A. With Jesus There Was Always Success.

      1. Not every person who was sick was healed by Jesus when He was here on planet earth.

      2. But everyone He attempted to heal was healed.

      3. You can unreservedly rely on divine healing when Jesus is involved in it—there are no failures with God!

      4. He attempted to heal only those who according to the will of God were to be healed.

      5. But He heals everyone He attempts to heal, EVERY TIME!

   B. With His Disciples and Apostles There Was Frequent Success.

      1. Successes:

         a. The lame man at the temple, Acts 3:2-7.

         b. Dorcus, Acts 9:37-41.

         c. The impotent man at Lystra, Acts 14:8-10.

         d. The soothsayer at Philippi, Acts 16:16-18.

         e. The diseased at Ephesus, Act 19:12.

         f. Eutychus, Acts 20:9, 10.

         g. The father of Publius, Acts 28:8.

      2. Failures:

         a. The man's son of Mark 9:18.

         b. Paul and his fleshly thorn, II Corinthians 12:7-10.

  c. Timothy and his stomach problems, I Timothy 5:23.

  d. Trophimus, II Timothy 4:20.

C. With The So-called Faith Healers There Is Little or No Real Success.

 1. With others:

  a. There are no documented cases known to us.

  b. Notice two quotes from Jerry Sholes who worked for a noted faith healer for over three years. In his book, *GIVE ME THAT PRIME-TIME RELIGION*, he makes the following statements:

   1.) *"I never saw anyone healed of anything and that bothered me. I saw people who had come expecting a healing and I saw the raw hope and desire in their eyes. If faith could have brought them up out of those wheelchairs, they would have come out and been ready to run a 50-yard dash, on the spot! It never happened.*

   Oh, once in a while someone would get up out of a wheelchair and limp off the stage. But, I'd seen them a day or two before get out of their wheelchair to get into cars or go into the restroom. They weren't total and incurable wheelchair cases," page 34.

   2.) *"In his "seminars," he prays for people after they have collectively pledged an amount that generally ranges from $1.5 million to $3 million. It is revealing to note that the pledge service comes first...then the healing line,"* page 161.

  c. And I ask, where are the greater works that Jesus promised to those who believe, John 14:12, *"Verily, verily, I say unto, He that believeth on me, the works that I do shall he do also; and greater works than these shall he do; because I go unto my Father."*

2. With themselves:
    a. Please name me five faith healers who have healed themselves when they have had a serious illness.
    b. I read about a divine healing couple that had to go to a doctor while they were holding a healing campaign. The female healer had "pink eye" which neither of them could cure.
    c. I do not know about you, but if a healer could not heal himself I could not have much faith in him.
    d. And have you noticed how many faith healers have died in your lifetime?
        1.) Since they would all have died of something, why didn't they just heal themselves and live forever?
        2.) And if it is a sin to have a disease as some of them proclaim then they all died in their sins, didn't they?
        3.) Where did they all go, to hell, to heaven?
3. With God.
    a. Because they do not take the time to discern the will of God for the sick one. They, by accident, do pray according to the will of God now and then.
    b. Because they blame everyone else but themselves for their failures.
    c. Because the outright denial of clear Biblical teaching shuts up God's ears to their prayers.
    d. Because they do it for fame and fortune when God's work is to be done for His honor and glory without charge!

D. With God There Is Nothing, But Success, Every Time.
  1. Always seek God's will for your life whether you're sick or well! Success is always found in the center of His will.
  2. God always heals each one He attempts to heal, and those He does not heal CANNOT BE HEALED BY ANYONE ELSE!

3. Go to the only divine healer, GOD, if you need to be healed—you'll never improve upon that practice! Read the whole story of Ahaziah, and what Elijah told him when he sought healing from a god other than God, II Kings 1:1-17, especially verse six which states, *"Thus saith the Lord, Is it not because there is not a God in Israel, that thou sendest to inquire of Baalzebub the god of Ekron? Therefore thou shalt not come down from that bed on which thou art gone up, but shall surely die."*

Scripture Text: James 5:13-16.

Theme: A More Excellent Way.

Title: Divine Healing Studied, How To Deal With Sickness, IV-c.

Introduction: As I have said before, I believe in divine healing, but not in divine healers. There is one divine healer, and that is the Lord God Almighty. As we approach this subject let us remember that James is one of the earliest Scripture writers. He is known for saying it like it is, and for his practical messages. Divine healing is possible today, but it should be done Scripturally. Most of the so-called divine healers prey upon the psychosomatically ill. Doctors say that at least fifty percent if not eighty percent of all illnesses are due to psychosomatic reasons. A divine healer therefore stands a fifty-fifty chance of supposedly healing anyone who trusts in him. Thus some will say, what is wrong with that? And we answer, it is anti-Scriptural, it is deceptive, and the divine healer is usually better healed than the supposed healed!

If this is true, then why do those with psychosomatic illnesses seek out those who will take advantage of them? The reason that religious sham artists can do this is that, those who are psychosomatically ill actually believe in their minds they are sick, and they have or will experience some type of actual illness in their bodies.

They are desperate people! They truly need help with their problem, but they do not need to be taken advantage of by those who are purporting to help them.

Anyone who would take advantage of a person who desperately needs help is the lowest of those who prey upon the helpless, the hopeless, and the hapless. Nevertheless, there are multitudes of those who seek to take advantage of the weak, the sick, and the poor. However, when you see this in religious circles you are seeing the worst of humanity at work!

Those using religion to take advantage of others are asking for divine judgment to be executed upon them. This is the reason we must be very careful as we attempt to use the gifts God has given to the Church. It would be much better to have never exercised a gift at all than to have exercised it wrongfully.

Ponder with me now what psychosomatic healing does:

1. It deceives the purported healed into believing he is healed when actually he has not been healed.
2. It insults God because it claims God's approval when He does not approve of it at all.
3. It lays the healer open to exposure, ridicule, and liable as soon as he is exposed as a fraud.
4. It discredits all true healing that takes place because it promotes doubt as it relates to Scriptural healing.
5. It causes true believers to stink in the eyes of the non-believers because they will believe that all believers are deceivers.
6. It makes the non-healed feel guilty because their lack of faith has kept the healing from taking place.
7. It leaves a trail of discouraged, and, sometimes critical, people who cry foul because they have been promised healing and it has not taken place.

God has made provision for healing according to His will in His Word for all of the Church Age. God gave the gifts to the Church to be used through the Church by the people of the Church.

Let us REMEMBER this as we study the lesson before us.

I. WHY DOES SICKNESS COME?
  A. Due To The Natural Consequence Of Sin.
    1. This deals with the effect sin has upon our bodies to bring about death.
        a. Sickness has its roots in sin, and since we are sinners by nature and by act sickness is going to touch us all at one time or another.
        b. The dying process is going to make some of us sick, and perhaps all of us.

      c. One sickness will be unto death unless Jesus comes first.
  2. This process can be accelerated by over indulging.
      a. Drinking brings sorrow, Proverbs 23:29-32.
      b. Gluttony brings sorrow, Proverbs 23:21.
      c. Immorality brings sorrow, Proverbs 5:3-5.
  3. When we break God's laws we accelerate the dying process original sin started.

B. Due To The Chastening Of The Lord.
  1. Notice these sins brought about sickness.
      a. The jealousy of Miriam produced leprosy, Numbers 12:10.
      b. Murmuring against Moses brought a plague, Numbers 16:49.
      c. Evil speaking brought fiery serpents, Numbers 21:5, 6.
      d. Adultery brought a plague upon those who were involved in this type of sin, Numbers 25:9.
      e. Abuse of the Lord's table brought sickness, weakness, and death, I Corinthians 11:30.
      f. These certainly are within the scope of affliction and sickness.
  2. God may use sickness to bring us closer to Him.
      a. Righteous Hezekiah is drawn closer to God, II Kings 20:1-7, and so was David, Psalms 32 and 51.
      b. Unrighteous Manasseh was drawn unto God, II Chronicles 33:11, 12.
      c. God chastens those whom He loves, Hebrews 12:6-8.

C. Due To The Glory Of God.
  1. Job pictures the test of faith made perfect through trails that God allowed Satan to bring upon him.
      a. He was singled out by God for the test: Job 1:8.
      b. He stood all that Satan gave out, Job 1:21.

- c. He was rewarded twofold by God, Job 42:12, 13.
- 2. The blind man was born blind that the works of God could be manifested, John 9:2, 3.
- 3. Paul demonstrated God's grace to endure an illness for the glory of God, II Corinthians 12:9
  - a. God does not heal every illness--we must accept that Scriptural and actual truth as an absolute fact!
  - b. But He does give grace to bear every illness He does not heal.
  - c. Anytime we are sick or afflicted we should ask God to point out its cause to us. God will not fail to help us to know this.

II. WHO IS THE INSTIGATOR OF SICKNESS?

- A. It Cannot Be God.
  - 1. Every good and every perfect gift is from Him, James 1:17.
  - 2. Everything God created was good, Genesis 1:31.
  - 3. God may use sickness for His glory, but He is not the instigator of sickness!
- B. It Is From Satan.
  - 1. Notice three cases from Scripture.
    - a. Satan is the one who put forth his hand to touch the property and person of Job.
      - 1.) Satan tempts God to touch Job and his property, but God cannot be tempted, Job 1:11, 12.
      - 2.) Job 2:4-7 says that it is Satan who smote Job.
    - b. Paul says that a messenger from Satan caused his affliction, II Corinthians 12:7.
    - c. Jesus says that Satan caused the woman to be bent over, Luke 13:16.

2. In fact, Satan has the power of death, Hebrews 2:14.
   a. He can do only as God allows, this is true.
   b. Nevertheless he does try to accuse every person of every sin he commits every time he commits a sin.
      1.) Revelation 12:10 calls him the accuser of the brethren, and he does this continually before God.
      2.) Satan uses God's Word to file charges against those who sin, Ezekiel 18:4.
      3.) He even contended for the body of Moses, Jude 9.
3. If it were not for the hedge of God we would all be consumed by Satan without a moment's hesitation.
4. We should not therefore blame God for our sicknesses—we should blame Satan. Sin gives Satan his power to inflict sickness and affliction. We should praise God for His hedge of protection—it is our sure haven of rest!

III. WHAT SHOULD WE DO WHEN SICKNESS COMES?

A. Be Scriptural.
   1. General comments:
      a. When the Word was authenticated divine healing ceased through the agency of man.
      b. It was a sign gift to authenticate the message and the messenger.
      c. James 5:13-16 gives us the proper procedure for this time period.
   2. The Scripture Studied.
      a. If it comes in the form of affliction, pray, 13.
         1.) This word means to suffer evil, to be vexed, troubled, dejected, or suffer hardship.

            - It includes physical and mental sufferings caused by life's problems.

- It does not deal primarily with organic illness.

- It deals primarily with psychosomatic illness.

2.) The way to deal with it is to pray to God.

- Notice that we can do this for ourselves.

- The Psalmist cries unto God, Psalm 61:1, 2.

- You do not need a faith healer for this!

- But what should you do? Ask God for wisdom, James 1:5.

- Prayer draws us to God, and He gives the answer we need to us.

- Usually the thing that keeps us from God also brings the affliction.

- No magical cure, just coming to Him in prayer with nothing between us, and our Redeemer.

- Prayer cures the psychosomatic illness when it is fervent and effectual.

- Yes, 50-80 percent of all sick people can be cured through prayer if the medical people are right in their estimation of those who are psychosomatically ill.

- And the sick person can pray for himself, so let him be found praying!

3.) The results will be that God will help the sick one to see the cause of his affliction, thus a cure in itself.

- Always pray, Thy will be done, Oh God.

- God will teach you to have faith in Him, and His ability to answer your prayer.

- I would be great in your eyes if I could heal you, but I'd rather be great in His eyes.

- It is Jesus who cures, Acts 3:16.

b. If it comes in the form of sickness, let him call for the elders of the Church, 14.

   1.) To be sick means to be without strength, to be weak, infirm, or feeble.

      - Jesus says heal the sick, Matthew 10:8.

      - Philippians 2:26, 27 states that Epaphroditus was sick unto death.

   2.) To deal with this type of sickness a person should call the elders (pastors) of the Church.

      - The elders' qualifications are found in I Peter 5:1-4, I Timothy 3:1-7, and Titus 1:5-9.

      - It is wise to follow God's pattern lest we offend Him by following some other voice.

   3.) The elders shall pray over him that is sick, and shall anoint him with oil in the name of the Lord.

      - No free will offering is to be taken.

      - No love offering is to be taken.

      - No public display of divine healing is to be seen other than that which could naturally be observed.

      - The prayer of faith is what heals, not the power of the healer.

      - The godly elders who have gathered seek God's will, then, pray according to it.

      - The anointing with oil probably symbolizes the work of the Holy Spirit.

   4.) The prayer of faith shall heal the sick one.

      - So often you hear, well you did not have enough faith for me to heal you.

      - Scripture says the elders prayed--it would be their lack of faith. Would agree to that?

5.) But remember it is not the will of God to heal everyone all the time.

- Paul prayed three times to be healed, II Corinthians 12:7-9.

- Paul left Trophimus sick at Miletus, II Timothy 4:20.

- Epaphroditus was sick unto death, Philippians 2:26, 27.

6.) The Lord shall raise up the sick one.

- God gets the glory here, not man.

- Who gets the most glory in faith healing as it is done today?

7.) Each sin must be confessed before healing can take place. Do you believe this to be Scripturally true?

- Confession brings restoration, I John 1:9,

- The word, heal means to restore to health.

- What else do we need to take care of affliction or our sickness? Any thing you have can be taken care of Scripturally. Do not be disappointed with man's inability to heal, be satisfied with God's absolute ability to heal!

B. Be Satisfied.

1. But I want to be cured, not satisfied—so say some!

   a. Isn't God's will important to you?

   b. Which is more important, God's will or your will? Be honest with yourself and God answering this question!

   c. Which will bring the greatest rewards and the most satisfaction? Answer this question before Almighty God!

Let me relate a real life incident to you that happened when I was preaching at a drive-in type of church service. I was preaching on Divine Healing in the evening service. After all the other cars had left I noticed a man and his wife in a station wagon beckoning to me.

I went over to them, and they introduced me to their son who could not move due to an earlier accident. They had just returned from Pittsburgh where they had sought healing for their son from a well-known faith healer. Their son returned home unhealed, and his parents returned home totally disappointed, discouraged, and perplexed. Thus they wanted some answers because they had been told that their lack of faith was the reason their son had not been healed. Wasn't the faith healer the one who had prayed? Wasn't it her inability to heal that left the boy unhealed? Why then were the parents blamed?

Needless to say, it took some time, and many Scriptures to demonstrate from the Word of God that God does not heal all sickness. They left praying, Thy will be done, Oh God! And they left with the peace of God in their hearts for the first time since the accident occurred for they now knew that His Grace was sufficient.

2. There is no cure apart from the will of God.

   a. Healers who prey upon the psychosomatically ill do not cure, they deceive, and they take advantage of those who are in disparate need of help.

   1.) They hide the problem, not cure the problem.

   2.) The problem will surface again in the same area or another area sooner or later.

   3.) And the supposedly healed are in worse shape than they were before for what hope do they have now?

   b. Healers who prey upon the truly sick are just as bad, if not worse. I say this because the person needing healing here could die.

   1.) They turn people from the truth unto a lie, and short change the seekers in the process.

   2.) They do not heal all that come, thus there are many disappointed people who have untold sorrow added to their sickness which had already taken its heavy toll on them.

3.) They cause the organically ill to suffer even more by adding guilt due to their supposed lack of faith.

4.) And they may even cause death when medications are forsaken because the sick ones think they have been cured when they have not been cured.

3. Test your faith healer by Biblical standards, not by the desires of your heart, or the false teachings of sinful men.

   a. Does he/she heal everyone he/she attempts to heal? Jesus did, Acts 10:38; Peter did, Acts 3:7; Philip did, Acts 8:6, 7; Paul did, Acts 14:9, 10, 28:8.

   b. Does he/she take a collection for each service?

   c. Does he/she heal all manner of sickness? Jesus did, Matthew 4:24; 9:35; the disciples did, Matthew 10:1; Peter did, Acts 5:16.

   d. Jesus can cure all manner of sickness both physical and mental. He can even cure the cause of sickness—sin. I offer to you Jesus who can cure every sickness even those unto spiritual death.

Scripture Text: James 5:13a.

Theme: A More Excellent Way.

Title: Divine Healing Studied, The Answer To Your Affliction, IV-d.

Introduction: In verse thirteen James introduces us to the subject of affliction. Affliction refers to the suffering we experience from the hardships this life offers us. Affliction is not an easy thing to bear, nor is it easy to understand; therefore many believers react wrongly to it. James tells us the secret of bearing well affliction—it is prayer! Yes, James says that it is prayer, real heartfelt prayer!

But you say, pastor that couldn't be right for I've tried it and it didn't work. However, I reply unto you that God says that prayer is the answer to affliction. The reason that we have blamed God for our affliction, and in our affliction is that we have not prayed aright. And the reason we become bitter at God, and our fellow man when we are afflicted is due to the fact that we have not properly prayed. Let us therefore learn how to pray properly about our affliction for Prayer Is The Answer To Our Affliction.

I. What Does It Mean To Be Afflicted?

   A. The Word Defined And Set In Context (κακοπαθεῖ).

      1. |When a person is afflicted he suffers persistent pain or distress.

      2. Affliction is usually associated with those who must suffer greatly.

      3. The suffering can be due to physical pain or mental stress or a combination of both.

      4. This type of suffering is not usually associated with sin and chastisement although it can be.

      5. In our context it refers to all the suffering associated with our lives simply because we are believers in the Lord Jesus Christ.

6. Thus James is speaking to you if you are suffering because you are a Christian who is trying to do the Lord's work.

B. The Word Studied In Seven Biblical Texts.

1. In II Timothy 1:8 it refers to those afflictions that come upon those who minister the Gospel (συγκάκοπαθησου).

   a. There are certain afflictions that always accompany the preaching of the Gospel.

   b. The devil is always at work using slanderers, liars, and gossipers to try to discredit those who preach the Gospel.

   c. You'll never stay long in the Lord's work if you are not willing to suffer the afflictions that accompany it.

2. In II Timothy 2:3 it refers to the hardness a good soldier of Jesus Christ must endure to carry out the orders of his commander-in-Chief (κακοπάθησου).

   a. This refers to the privations a follower of Jesus must suffer such as: being away from home a lot, suffering assaults from the enemy, having to forsake all for his Master's cause, and experiencing fatigue, exhaustion, and loneliness.

   b. Being a Christian is no position for a weak hearted person to apply for at any time.

   c. Many hard things will come his way, but he is to suffer them for the cause of Christ like a soldier would suffer hardships for his commander.

3. In II Timothy 2:9, it refers to the trouble a good child of God suffers as an evildoer simply because he seeks to do God's will for his life (κακοπαθῶ).

   a. Now many people will consider you an evildoer if you seek first the kingdom of God and His righteousness.

   b. Others will consider you an evildoer if you try to deal justly and equally with all men.

c. And they will do everything in their power to see that trouble comes your way because of your efforts.

d. In fact, you'll be treated like an evildoer when actually you are doing God's will.

4. In II Timothy 4:5 it refers to the affliction one must endure to avoid succumbing to false teachings (κακοπάθησον).

   a. You take your stand for Christ, and oppose false teachings and you'll suffer.

   b. When you speak out against homosexuality, drunkenness, dope addiction, immorality, smoking, false doctrine, and social injustice you'll be afflicted with multiple tongue-lashings, and perhaps physical abuse also.

   c. But Oh child of God, it is all part of your lot with Christ. Count it all glory when you suffer for His cause!

5. In Hebrews 11:25 it refers to the affliction coming upon the one who identifies with a supposed inferior race by those of a supposed superior race (συγκακουχεῖσθαι).

   a. When Moses was considered an Egyptian he was well treated by the Egyptians although he was a Hebrew.

   b. But when he chose to identify with the Hebrew nation he began to suffer affliction.

   c. However, praise God he considered that affliction of greater value to him than all the riches of Egypt.

6. In James 5:10 it refers to the suffering endured by the prophets of God for preaching God's Holy Word (κακοπαθείας).

   a. Now you may not be a preacher of God's Word, and think you are safe.

   b. But for your own benefit remind yourself of all the prophets have endured, Hebrews 11:32-38.

   c. Then take them as your example if you are afflicted in this present time.

7. In James 5:13a it refers to all those different circumstances of life we must go through simply because we are believers.
C. The Word Applied.
  1. Now we must ask ourselves what effect, if any, affliction will have upon us.
  2. Let me list just a few of the effects it will have:
    a. It shall weigh heavily upon our minds and hearts.
    b. It shall press upon our soul and spirit until both become dejected.
    c. It shall injury our bodies psychosomatically, and actually.
    d. It shall disrupt our whole manner of living.
    e. It shall destroy our will to continue on for our Lord and Savior.
    f. It shall tear down the good relationships that have taken years to develop.
  3. Therefore we cannot afford to react wrongly to affliction.
  4. What should we do then if we are afflicted? PRAY!

II. HOW SHOULD WE REACT WHEN WE ARE AFFLICTED?
  A. We Should Pray Because It May Be God's Will To Remove It.
    1. We'll never know this until we spend enough time in prayer to find out.
    2. Through prayer we discern the will of God as it relates to our affliction.
    3. Then once the will of God is discerned we can pray with certainty that our prayer will be answered and our affliction will be lifted.
    4. But who wants to spend that much time in prayer?
    5. The one who wants to deal Biblically with his affliction, the one who wants, above all else, to know God's will about his affliction.

6. But oh what a joy it is to see God remove an affliction after we have prayed unto Him about it.
7. Do you see why God says, LET HIM PRAY?

B. We Should Pray Because It May Be God's Will To Give Us The Victory Over It.
1. We'll never know this until we spend enough time in prayer to find out.
2. God may desire to leave the affliction upon us or around us so that He can demonstrate His grace through us.
3. Once we understand this, the affliction will become a joy as we see how God has taken the thing that troubled us, and has given us complete victory over it even though it stares us in the face every day of our life.
4. Only prayer will give us the ability to discern this, and then give us the strength to experience it.
5. But who wants to pray that long and hard?
6. The person who doesn't want to be overcome by his affliction when it is God's will not to remove it, but to overcome it.

C. We Should Pray Because It May Not Be God's Will To Remove It, Nor To Give Us Victory Over It—we may have to endure it by His grace.
1. Now probably no one wants to pray until he finds this out.
2. Nevertheless, we had better find out before it destroys us, before our confidence in God weakens, and before our trust in the promises of God fades.
3. You see, there are afflictions which God may ask us to endure, He may not remove them, He may not give us victory over them—He may simply give us the grace to bear them even though daily we suffer because of them.
   a. I will cite only one passage, and if it does not convince you of what I have said, then I do not believe you are allowing the Holy Spirit to speak to your heart and your

mind. I cite II Corinthians 12:7-10. We'll develop this more, later.

    b. I would have used a greater example or a clearer example if I could, but this example, humanly speaking is all sufficient in and of itself.

4. Now we need to pray more about this kind of affliction than any other kind of affliction.

5. It is the most difficult kind to bear because we must have God's grace in our lives every moment of our lives, and that, just to keep our sanity.

6. James asks if any among you are afflicted? Then he says, let the afflicted ones be continually in prayer as it relates to their affliction so that they'll know what God's will is pertaining to the affliction, and then avail themselves to the grace of God so that they'll be able to bear the affliction according to the will of God and unto the glory of God.

7. Are you afflicted? Have You Prayed? Then Do It Now So That God Can Begin To Answer Your Prayer.

Scripture Text: James 5:13b.

Theme: A More Excellent Way.

Title: Divine Healing Studied, How To Prolong Your Cheerfulness, IV-e.

Introduction: Our last study taught us a very important, but very simple truth: if anyone is afflicted among you he should pray. That simple truth had to be expounded before we could really put it into practice. I trust that you have put it into practice already. Now in this lesson we face another one of those simple truths from James. He very simply asks, "Is Any Merry?" Then he says, "let him sing psalms!" Anyone can do that, right? Before you answer I want to study this portion of God's Word so that when you answer you'll have all the facts before you. And at the end of this lesson we are going to have a quiz on what we have studied, so you had better pay close attention. Listen then as I tell you what you must do first if you are to prolong your cheerfulness.

I. UNDERSTAND WHAT YOU ARE TO DO.

   A. For James Asks, "Is Any Merry," that is, among you?

      1. Now to answer that question you must understand what he has asked you.

      2. He is asking you if your mind and heart have teamed up so that a cheerful attitude has been created in you (εὐθυμεῖ-3p/s/present/indicative).

         a. Your mind must feed your soul good thoughts before it can respond in a positive manner.

         b. Your soul will express a cheerful attitude if your mind feeds it good material continually.

      3. He is asking if you have taken courage to the point that you actually feel good about yourself, and the will of God for yourself.

      4. He is asking you if you are so free of the circumstance of life that you are actually living above it even as you are living in it.

5. But you ask, how can I be cheerful so long as I live on planet earth?
6. And I reply, by laying hold of a promise of God that pertains to your circumstance.
   a. In Acts 27:22 Paul exhorts the centurion, the master of the ship, and the owner of the ship (27:11) to be of good cheer even though they were about to lose everything to a storm called Euroclydon (27:14.
   b. He bases his exhortation to be of good cheer upon the promise from God that no lives would be lost, Acts 27:23-25.
   c. He uses the same word (εὐθυμεῖν-James 5:13 and εὐθυμεῖτε-Acts 27:25) that James uses when he asks if any is merry among you.
7. We therefore conclude that we can be merry or cheerful by laying hold of and acting upon a promise God has given pertaining to our circumstance.
   a. Our minds must feed our souls the promise of God continually before the soul can be cheerful.
   b. Our souls in turn will become cheerful or merry as they feed upon the Word of God.
   c. But how do we prolong that cheerfulness which has been created by a promise of God?

B. Let Him Sing Psalms (ψαλλέτε).
1. The word, sing and the word psalms both come from one Greek word which means to sing praise accompanied by music.
   a. To sing means to verbalize musically—we all understand what this means. First speak the word, Hallelujah. Now sing it as it is sung in the Hallelujah Chorus, and notice the difference!
   b. To praise means to express grateful approval for benefits received.

1.) The word translated psalms has the root meaning, to praise.

2.) The Psalmist says, *"Let everything that hath breath praise the Lord,"* Psalm 150:6.

3.) And we understand that praising the Lord is pleasant, Psalm 135:3.

4.) The Psalms are filled with praise unto the Lord, Psalm 148:1-7.

5.) But we are to praise the Lord in psalms, hymns, and spiritual songs also.

c. And to be accompanied by God inspired music builds us up in the Holy Faith as we praise our great God for the beneficial promise He has given us.

d. Say Hallelujah! Then sing Hallelujah! Now sing Hallelujah accompanied by music. Are you beginning to see that James knows what he is talking about?

3. James commands us to sing praises unto God when we are cheerful or merry because it will prolong our cheerfulness (ψαλλέτε-3p/s/present/ imperative).

a. As long as we are truly praising we will be cheerful.

b. As soon as we become cheerful or merry we should begin to sing praises unto God and these praises should be accompanied by music so that we may prolong our period of cheerfulness.

c. Now that we know how to answer James, and what we should do, let me instruct you how to do it Biblically.

II. DO IT BIBLICALLY.

A. Your Singing Should Be Based On The Word Of God, Colossians 3:16.

1. Notice that Paul exhorts us to let the Word of Christ dwell in us richly in all wisdom teaching and admonishing one

another in psalms, that is the Word of God; in hymns, all good hymns are based on the Bible; and spiritual songs, which are God centered.

    a. If you are cheerful, sing only God enriched songs.

    b. If you are cheerful, play only God inspired and Christ exalting music.

2. If you are cheerful, and want to stay that way, compliment the promise of God that made you cheerful by singing songs that are Word enriched.

B. Your Singing Should Be Intelligent Singing, I Corinthians 14:15.

1. Paul gives the Corinthians several guidelines in this verse, one of which is: sing with the understanding.

2. If you cannot understand what you are singing, do not sing it or listen to it!

    a. You could be singing to the devil.

    b. You could be saying nothing at all that would help, in fact, you may actually doing yourself great harm!

    c. You could be singing a good song, but missing its message completely.

3. Understanding enhances what is being sung, and helps lift you up.

    a. A song done poorly in which the words are Biblical and understandable is much better than the greatest rendition of any song in which the words were not understandable!

    b. Christian music should be written and sung to the glory of God, not to display a singer's talent.

    c. However, a great song sung by a very talented person will give God the glory, and will bless the hearer's heart.

4. Study each song you sing so that you'll know what song compliments what promise of God you are relying upon.

5. Then sing it with complete understanding, and it will help prolong your cheerfulness.

C. Your Singing Should Be By The Spirit, Ephesians 5:18, 19a.
   1. Here Paul tells us to be continually being filled with the Holy Spirit.
      a. We do that by confessing each sin as soon as we commit it, thus we empty ourselves of sin by allowing God to cleanse us from all confessed sins, I John 1:9.
      b. When we are cleaned from all unrighteousness, then we are filled with the Holy Spirit.
      c. We are not indwelt once again, but we are filled once again with the Holy Spirit.
      d. The indwelling is once for all time while the filling is as often as we sin, confess it, and are cleansed of it.
   2. Now flowing out of that Spirit filled life will be a ministry that will prolong your cheerfulness because you are speaking to yourself in psalms, hymns, and spiritual songs.
   3. The Spirit filled person will allow the Holy Spirit to take the promise of God that has made him cheerful, and cause him to sing psalms with his understanding so that his cheerfulness is prolonged.
   4. Aren't you impressed with the simplicity of James?
D. Your Singing Should Be From The Heart, Ephesians 5:19b.
   1. Now when you put your heart into your singing, and the musical accompaniment enriches your singing which is Biblical in content you will become so happy that you will continue to remain cheerful.
   2. Isn't God great? Only He could give you such a simple plan to keep you cheerful, and may I suggest that it will be much less expansive than going to a therapist.
   3. But you say, Sure that's great on my good days, but what about all those other kind of days?

III. DO IT WITH ALL YOUR HEART AS UNTO THE LORD.
   A. As You Experience The Happy Times Of This Everyday Life
      1. Now I'll be the first to admit that it is easier to be cheerful when everything is going great.
         a. I will also admit that you can have a hard time being cheerful even on a great day.
         b. So please be aware of the fact that the devil can and does hinder our cheerfulness even when all things are going great.
      2. However, if you want to prolong your cheerfulness even when you're happy, then sing praises unto God that are accompanied by good music.
   B. As You Experience The Humdrum Doldrums Of This Everyday Life.
      1. The humdrum life is characterized by not anything outstanding happening: neither good, nor bad.
      2. It's the same old life day in and day out.
      3. Who could be cheerful in a situation like this? Every believer! Every day! All the days of his life!
      4. Anyone of God's great promises could lift you up, and make you cheerful, I John 5:13, *"These things have I written unto you that believe on the name of the Son of God; that ye may know that ye have eternal life, and that ye may believe on the name of the Son of God."*
      5. Doesn't that excite you? Then sing this first verse of *Blessed Assurance, "Blessed assurance, Jesus is mine! O what a foretaste of glory divine! Heir of salvation, purchase of God, Born of the Spirit, washed in His blood. This is my story, this is my song, Praising my Savior all the day long; this is my story, this my song:*

      Praising my Savior all the day long." LIVING HYMNS, stanza one, page 51.

6. Put on a good musical rendition of this song, or accompany yourself so that your cheerfulness is prolonged.

C. As You Experience The Afflictions Of This Everyday Life.
   1. Here is where we are ready to put to the test that which we have learned.
   2. Can we find a promise in the Bible that will minister to our lack of cheerfulness?
   3. How about Hebrews 13:5, 6, *"Let your conversation be without covetousness; and be content with such things as ye have: for he hath said, I will never leave thee, nor forsake thee. So that we may boldly say, The Lord is my helper, and I will not fear what man shall do unto me."*
   4. Will you, on your own, read the above verse, and then find an appropriate song to sing? Read the words over and over until you understand what message the song is conveying to you. Next, sing it without music. Now, add the music. You are now ready to put your heart and soul into it as you allow the Holy Spirit to lead you as you sing unto the Lord! This is your test!

Scripture Text: James 5:14.

Theme: A More Excellent Way.

Title: Divine Healing Studied, Sickness Defined, IV-f.

Introduction: I want to get started on this lesson by setting forth three main points. The first point deals with defining sickness so that we know what James is talking about. The second point zeros in on why sickness comes. And the third point identifies the instigator of sickness. This will be an expansion of some material that we introduced to you earlier, but in simple outline form. Now we need all of this information before us before we ever begin to study divine healing. Please take the time to listen carefully as we study this introductory material—it will help you keep all sickness in its proper prospective. Without this information you'll never be able to understand sickness, nor what to do when sickness comes your way. Notice then:

I. HOW WE SHOULD DEFINE THE WORD, SICKNESS.

   A. The Basic Meaning Of The Word, Sickness.

   1. The word sickness ('ασθενεῖ) has several related meanings that we need to study.

      a. The word means to be without strength, when we are sick there is a lack of strength.

      b. It means to be weak, when we are sick we become weak due to the toll it takes on us.

      c. It means to be feeble, when we are sick we become feeble in body, and sometimes in mind also.

      d. And it means to be in ill health, when we are in ill health we say that we are sick.

   2. The basic idea then in this word centers upon the results of ill health rather than identifying the cause of it.

   3. Thus James is asking if any of the brothers and sisters in Christ have progressed in their ill health to the point that they are unable to carry on with the normal activities of life.

4. In other words he is asking them if they are confined to the bed, the house, or the hospital.

B. The Scriptural Usage Of The Word, Sickness.

1. We learn from Mark 6:56 that Jesus was in the business of healing the sick ('ασθενούντας).

2. We learn from Luke 4:40 that those who were sick had divers diseases ('ασθενούντας νόσοις).

3. We learn from John 4:46, 47 that the nobleman's son was sick unto the point of death (ἠσθένει).

4. We learn from John 5:3, 7 that sickness ('αθενούντων-impotence) expressed itself in blindness, lameness, and paralysis.

5. We learn from John 6:2 that sickness is related to disease ('ασθενούτων-diseased).

6. And from John 11:1-3, 14 we learn that Lazarus died of his sickness.

7. Thus when James asked the brothers and sisters of his day if any was sick among them they understood what he said: Do any of you have an organic problem which has taken your strength away so that you are confined to the bed or need help to get about?

C. The Conclusions We Must Draw.

1. This word is used in other ways in Scripture such as in Romans 4:19, 14:1, where it refers to weakness in faith.

2. But when it is used in conjunction with people's physical problems it always refers to the effects of some organic disorder.

3. Thus we conclude that James is referring to physical sickness in 5:14.

II. WHY DOES SICKNESS COME?

Yes, I have given you similar material before, but then it was in bare outline form. In this lesson we put some more meat on the skeleton so be sure to not skip over it. A careful study will benefit you much!

I also have given it here because I have found that most people do not get it all the first time, nor are they inclined to go back to a previous passage to refresh their memories.

May I therefore build upon what I have already taught you, and may you drink deeply from this expanded review of this very important material.

   A. Due To The Natural Consequences Of Sin!
      1. This deals with the effect sin has had upon our bodies as it seeks to bring about physical death.
         a. Do you remember that God told Adam that he would die the day he ate of the tree of the knowledge of good and evil, Genesis 2:16, 17?
         b. The dying process started there was threefold: he died spiritually at that moment, he began to die physically at that very moment also, and he would die eternally as soon as physical death occurred.
         c. We focus upon the fact that we can see sin's effect in the succeeding generations.
            1.) Now God created man with the potential of living forever, *"And the Lord God said, Behold, the man is become as one of us, to know good and evil: and now, lest he put forth his hand, and take also of the tree of life, and eat, and live forever,"* Genesis 3:22.
            2.) However, as soon as sin entered into the world, so did death, *"Wherefore, as by one man sin entered into the world, and death by sin; and so death passed upon all men, for that all have sinned,"* Romans 5:12.

3.) We all die because we have all sinned, Romans 3:23, *"For all have sinned, and come short of the glory of God."*

- Our wages for sinning is death, Romans 6:23.

- When a person dies physically, he dies because he has sinned, that's the penalty for sinning even if he has had his sins forgiven.

- Sickness is a part of that dying process for it has it roots in sin.

- The dying process is going to make all of us sick now and then, but one of our sicknesses will be unto death unless the Lord raptures us first.

4.) I can trace the effect of sin upon mankind from creation until the time of Moses.

- The average lifespan of man from Adam to Noah was 857 years over a period of ten generations.

- But from Noah to Peleg it had dropped to 577 years in only a period of another five generations.

- Then with the passing of another five generation, from Peleg to Abraham, the average lifespan was down to 212 years.

- And from Abraham to Moses it had slipped to 120 years, Deuteronomy 34:7.

- But in Psalm 90:10 Moses tells us that God had lower the average age of a person to seventy to eighty years.

5.) Do you see how sin has been shortening the lifespan of mankind throughout his history?

6.) I sincerely believe it would have annihilated the human race had God not stepped in to stop it.

2. This natural process of dying however can be accelerated by various sins, or accidents.
    a. You see we all are going to die because of some sickness, that's the natural process set in motion by sin.
    b. Even if we are godly people and pure people all the days of our lives—we will still die of some sickness.
    c. But we can hasten death by living deeply in sin.
        1.) Yes I know of some who have lived in sin, and lived long lives compared with others who did not live deeply in sin.
        2.) But the bottom line is that their lives were shortened, and they would have lived longer had they not lived so deeply in sin.
        3.) Thus we cannot compare shortness or longevity of life with one another, but only with God's will for a life.
        4.) Sin shortens the life God has given us to live.
    d. Thus when we break God's laws we accelerate the dying process original sin started.
    e. One word of caution as we conclude this point, please remember that what a person gets from his ancestral gene pool determines to a large extent, humanly speaking, how well he lives and how long he lives. SOME VERY GOOD PEOPLE DO DIE YOUNG!
B. Due To The Chastening Hand Of The Lord Being Upon Us.
    1. Notice that these sins brought about sickness.
        a. Jealousy brought leprosy upon Miriam the sister of Moses, Numbers 12:10.
            1.) She and Aaron spake against Moses, Numbers 12:1.
            2.) They said that they were just as spiritual as Moses was, Numbers 12:2.

3.) This angered the Lord to the point that He begins the chastening process, Numbers 12:3-9.

4.) Miriam became leprous for seven days, Numbers 12:10-15.

b. Murmuring brought a plague upon those who complained about the leadership of Moses, Numbers 16:49.

1.) Korah lead a rebellion against Moses charging him with taking too much upon himself, Numbers 16:1-3

2.) God judged Korah and his friends worthy of death; therefore the ground opened up and swallowed them, Numbers 16:31-33.

3.) And to compound the matter the children of Israel complained against God who then sent a plague among them, Numbers 16:41, 46, 49.

c. Speaking against God and Moses brought fiery serpents among the complainers, Numbers 21:5, 6.

1.) But when they repented of their sin God made a provision whereby they could be delivered, Numbers 21:7-9.

2.) Would to God that God's people would learn from these examples that we are to refrain from speaking unjustly against God's servants.

d. Adultery brought a plague upon Israel, Numbers 25:9.

1.) Israel committed whoredom with the daughters of Moab, and with their gods, Numbers 25:1-3.

2.) This caused the fierce anger of the Lord to be upon them, Numbers 25:3b-5.

3.) But Phinehas turned away the fierce anger of the Lord and stayed the plague by his action, Numbers 25:10, 11.

e. Abuse of the Lord's Table brought sickness, weakness, and death upon the believers at Corinth, I Corinthians 11:30, *"For this cause many are weak and sickly among you, and many sleep."*

f. All of these are certainly in the scope of our word, sickness.
2. God chastens those who are His own, Hebrews 12:6-8.
　　a. Some sickness is due to the chastening hand of the Lord being upon us, but not all sickness is due to this reason.
　　b. However, we must learn to respond Scripturally to chastening when it occurs.
　　c. Thus we take time to point out the proper responses.
　　　1.) We are not to despise the chastening of the Lord for if we respond properly it will make a better person of us, and it will cause us to respect God more, Hebrews 12:5a.
　　　2.) We are not to faint when we are rebuked by the Lord for it will never be more than we can bear, and the test will strengthen us in the Lord, Hebrews 12:5b.
　　　3.) We are to understand that God chastens only those He loves for every loving father chastens his erring children to demonstrate his love for them, Hebrews 12:6a.
　　　4.) We are to comprehend that God scourgeth every son that He receives so that each son will know that sin always has a penalty to pay, and so that each son will not have to pay so many penalties for sin, Hebrews 12:6b.
　　　5.) We must learn to endure chastening because God is dealing with us as any good father would. We are either chastened by the Lord, or punished by the devil, Hebrews 12:7.
　　　6.) We must realize that if we do not receive chastening that we are not children of God for chastening from God equals son-ship while no chastening equals illegitimacy, Hebrews 12:8.

> 7.) We are to accept that the end goal of chastening is the peaceful fruit of righteousness whereby we know the difference between the bitter fruit of sin, and the peaceful fruit of righteousness, Hebrews 12:11. We therefore should always respond positively and immediately to the chastening hand of the Lord—its purpose is to bring us back into a right relationship with God!

C. Due To The Glory Of God!

I must interject a few words into our study at this point. The other day I was channel surfing on television when a certain speaker gained my attention by saying that no one should ever go around sick saying that it was to the glory of God. Had he ever read, John 11:4? Had he read it, and now is denying it? Does he not know that Jesus is speaking these words to us? Did he not hear Jesus say that Lazarus' sickness was for the glory of God? Well, if this passage is not enough to convince you that some sickness is for the glory of God, then I am going to use three other passages of Scripture to prove that that man did not know what he was talking about.

1. Job pictures the test of faith made perfect, Job 1:1-2:11.

   a. Job wasn't informed by God as to what was going on, or why it was going on.

   b. He didn't have a Bible he could read, and learn how God works.

   c. He was without a true friend from whom he could secure a solace for his heart.

   d. He had not even one family member to comfort him for even his wife gave uncomforting advice.

   e. He was singled out by God for the test without his knowledge, Job 1:8.

   f. He was personally attacked by Satan as it pertains to his possessions, his family, and his person, Job 1:12, 2:6.

      1.) In one day he lost seven sons and three daughters.

2.) In one day he lost seven thousand sheep, three thousand camels, five hundred yoke of oxen, five hundred she asses, and at least one house.

   3.) In one other day Job was smitten with sore boils from the sole of his foot unto the crown of his head, Job 2:7.

  g. And he had to endure it all until the test was over, but when the test was over God rewarded him, Job 42:12, 13.

   1.) His so-called friends were rebuked by God, Job 42:7-9.

   2.) His extended family, and friends gave him much wealth, Job 42:11.

   3.) And God doubled his possessions and family.

      - Doubled the animals.

      - Ten kids in heaven, and ten kids on earth.

  h. Now I want you to read the book of Job seven times carefully before you tell me that this sickness, and this affliction wasn't for the glory of God!

  i. It was for God's glory, it lasted until God said it was over, and struggle as Job would with God it wasn't over until God said it was over. No one could have healed him until the test was over! Hear also what Jesus said of Lazarus' sickness, Jn. 11:4.

2. The blind man of John 9:2, 3 was born blind so that the works of God could be manifested.

  a. Did you hear what Jesus said to His disciples?

   1.) This man did not sin, nor did his parents sin to cause his blindness.

   2.) This man was born blind that the works of God should be made manifest.

  b. Did you hear what his parents said, *"he is of age; ask him,"* John 9:21, 23.

1.) From the time of his birth until the moment Jesus healed him—he had been blind!

2.) He could not have been healed before that very moment because the very moment of his healing was ordained by God so that it would manifest the works of God!

3.) And truly the works of God were manifested when Jesus healed him, John 9:30, 32, 36-38.

  c. Please read the ninth chapter of John prayerfully, submit yourself to the ministry of the Holy Spirit, and then confess with the blind man who was healed that this man was born blind for the glory of God, and that he stayed blind unto the works of God could be manifested.

3. Paul demonstrated God's grace to endure a thorn in the flesh, II Corinthians 12:9.

  a. Paul was given a thorn in the flesh, the messenger of Satan.

1.) This messenger was from Satan, II Corinthians 12:7.

2.) Its purpose was to buffet Paul or discourage him from doing the will of God.

3.) It is described as a thorn or something that irritates continually.

4.) And it was given to him by Satan, but it was allowed by God.

  b. Paul prays that God will remove it three times, II Corinthians 12:8.

1.) I know of no better prayer warrior than Paul, humanly speaking.

2.) There was a divine purpose at work in God's refusal to remove the thorn, II Corinthians 12:7a, 9a.

  c. But God says, *"My grace is sufficient for thee: for my strength is made perfect in weakness."*

          1.) God is going to show everyone how sufficient His grace is to overcome physical weakness.

          2.) The weaker Paul is to overcome his weakness the greater is God's grace shown as he overcomes through patient endurance.

    d. Paul's response was, *"Most gladly therefore will I rather glory in my infirmities, that the power of Christ may rest upon me, II Corinthians 12:9b.*

    e. Would you please take notice of the pleasures that Paul could claim as his because he took this response, II Corinthians 12:10?

          1.) Therefore he takes Pleasure in Infirmities.

          2.) Therefore he takes Pleasure in Reproaches.

          3.) Therefore he takes Pleasure in Necessities.

          4.) Therefore he takes Pleasure in Persecutions.

          5.) Therefore he takes Pleasure in Distresses.

    f. Paul realized that he was stronger when he was weak, in and of himself, because then he had the full power of God working in him and through him.

    g. Now I ask you, Did Paul's thorn in the flesh remain with him?

    h. Did the thorn in his flesh bring honor and glory to God? Yes, it most certainly did!

    i. How then could anyone say that it is a sin to remain sick, and/or afflicted in cases such as this? No One Could!

    j. This only could be said of those who are living in sin, and the chastening hand of God is upon them.

4. Some concluding statements concerning this topic.

    a. God does not heal every illness or all illnesses, please remember this!

          1.) He didn't do it when He was here on earth, and He doesn't do it now.

- 2.) He heals only those who according to God's will are to be healed, then and now!
- 3.) Evidently, some who could be healed aren't because they have not responded to God's will for their lives.
  - b. But He does give the grace to bear all illness that is unto His honor and glory.
  - c. Anytime we are sick we should ask God to point out its cause.
    - 1.) If it is due to a natural cause, pray about it and treat it as best you can.
    - 2.) If it is due to sin, pray about it and confess it unto God asking HIM to forgive you of your sin!
    - 3.) If it is due to God seeking glory from it, pray about it and bear it unto His Glory.

III. WHO IS THE INSTIGATOR OF SICKNESS?

- A. It Cannot Be God.
  1. Everything God Created Was Good, Genesis 1:31, *"And God saw every thing that he had made, and, behold, it was very good."*
     - a. This was at the end of His creative work.
     - b. Nothing was made (created) after this statement.
     - c. Therefore nothing bad, evil, or worthless can come from Him.
  2. Every good and perfect gift is from Him, James 1:17, *"Every good gift and every perfect gift is from above, and cometh down from the Father of lights, with whom is no variableness, neither shadow of turning."*
     - a. If it is good, then it came from God.
     - b. If it is perfect, then it came from God.
     - c. Only when man touches the good things God has given with evil hands do they become bad.

  d. And the devil is the one who tempts man to corrupt the good things God has given to man.

  e. Just read how Satan dealt with Eve in the Garden of Eden, Genesis 3:1-5.

 3. Why then do we have sickness? Because God allows Satan to make us sick so that His divine purposes can be fulfilled.

 4. And as a final reminder let us read James 1:13, 14, *"Let no man say when he is tempted, I am tempted of God: for God cannot be tempted with evil, neither tempteth he any man: but every man is tempted, when he is drawn away of his own lust, and enticed."*

B. It Is From Satan.

 1. Notice three cases from Scripture that we have already studied, but with a different purpose in mind.

  a. Satan is the one who put forth his hand to touch the property, the family, and the person of Job.

   1.) His property, Job 1:6-19. We ask that you read this portion of Scripture over very carefully for we will not study it again since it does not relate directly to our purpose. However, there would be an extremely high amount of stress involved here.

   2.) His family of seven sons and three daughters was lost all at once, Job 1:2, 18, 19. Here again there would be anxiety and stress. Satan works in this area more than we could ever realize, that is, without God's help.

   3.) His person, Job 2:1-8.

    - Notice that God asks Satan if he has considered Job worthy of being tested, Job 2:2, 3.

    - Satan challenges God to touch Job's bone and flesh, 2:5.

    - God replies, *"Behold he is in thine hand, but save his life,"* 2:6.

- *"So went Satan forth from the presence of the Lord, and smote Job with sore boils from the sole of his foot unto his crown," 2:7.*

    4.) Is there any doubt now? If there is, then read this whole section over two or three times, and let the Holy Spirit have His way in your mind and heart.

  b. Jesus says that Satan caused the woman of Luke 13:16 to be bent over, *"And ought not this woman being a daughter of Abraham, whom Satan hath bound, lo, these eighteen years, be loosed from this bond on the Sabbath day?"*

    1.) Is there any room for doubt relating to this passage?

    2.) Satan is the one who causes sickness!

  c. Paul says that a messenger from Satan caused his affliction, II Corinthians 12:7, *"And lest I be exalted above measure through the abundance of the revelations, there was given to me a thorn in the flesh, the messenger of Satan to buffet me, lest I should be exalted above measure."*

    1.) Who caused Paul's affliction? Satan!

    2.) Who causes our afflictions and sickness? Satan, both directly and indirectly!

2. In fact, Satan has the power of death until God destroys death, Hebrews 2:14, *"Forasmuch then as the children are partakers of flesh and blood, he also himself likewise took part of the same; that through death he might destroy him that had the power of death, that is, the devil."*

  a. Please remember that he must have permission from God to take a life, Job 2:6.

  b. Nevertheless he is called the accuser of the brethren, Revelation 12:10.

    1.) The Scripture says, *"the soul that sinneth, it shall die,"* Ezekiel 18:4.

> 2.) And Satan tries to claim every sinner. Why, he even contended for the body of Moses, Jude 1:9.

3. If it were not for the hedge of God we would all be consumed by Satan, Job 1:9, 10, 2:4-6, I Peter 5:8.

    a. Satan is to be blamed for all sickness, even to some extent, to those we inflict upon ourselves. However, there is always an element of human responsibility in each sinful act.

    b. But God uses sickness, brought about by Satan, to bring about death which is the penalty for sin, to bring us back to Him when we backslide, and for His honor and glory as He sustains us through affliction and sickness, gives us victory over these, and ultimately delivers us from death itself! HALLELUJAH, PRAISE THE LORD!

Scripture Text: James 5:14, 15.

Theme: A More Excellent Way.

Title: Divine Healing Studied, What Is A Sick Person To Do, IV-g.

Introduction: We have made tremendous progress since we first introduced this topic of study to you. In that lesson we learned what James was referring to when he asked if any among you is sick. We then proceeded to outline for you why sickness comes. And finally we identified the instigator of all sickness. Now in this lesson we get into the text a little further so that we can tell the sick one among us what to do when he is sick. This is very important because sick people need to know what to do, how to do it, and when to do it. James carefully lays all of this out for us so that we'll know how to do that which is pleasing to God when we are sick. Listen as he tells us first of all:

I. WHAT THE SICK PERSON IS TO DO!

   A. He Is To Call For The Elders Of The Church To Which He Belongs.

      1. The spiritual status of the sick one—he is a believer.

         a. James wrote this epistle to the twelve tribes that were scattered abroad, 1:1.

         b. He calls them brethren and beloved brethren many times, 1:2, 16, 19, 2:1, 14, 3:1.

         c. He now asks these believers if they have any sick ones among them.

      2. The church to which he belongs is the local body of believers (ἐκκλήσιασ).

         a. But you may ask how I know he was a church member, and I reply that the Lord told me that He adds to the Church daily those who are saved, Acts 2:47c.

         b. Now it is true that some believers are not local church members in that they do not have their names on any local church roll---they are however members of the Church Universal.

c. But we also know that the Church Universal does not observe the ordinances nor does it hold church meetings.

   d. Thus I would certainly encourage you to add your name to the church roll at the church where the Lord has already added you and set you as it has pleased Him, I Corinthians 12:18.

   - Now if you'll allow me to digress for a moment or two I would like to ask you , before God, if the Church of Jesus Christ would have a much greater and more lasting impact on the world if every person who is a born-again believer would find their divinely ordained place in the local church where God has set them, and then serve God in that capacity with all their heart, soul, spirit, mind, and strength so long as God wills?

   - If it would, then we must seek to carry out equally each Scriptural duty listed in the Great Commission to receive the maximum return on the Gospel seed that is being sown.

   - Thus we must simultaneously empathize soul-winning until every lost soul has come to the saving knowledge of Jesus Christ, we must empathize that every believer should follow the Lord's command to be Scripturally baptized, and we must empathize that every baptized believer should unite with the God honoring local church to which God added them so that they may be taught to observe the ALL THINGS that Jesus has commanded them to be taught.

   - Now this type of regenerate church membership will be spiritually equipped and mentally prepared to reap any and every ripened harvest field that is provided by God in any and every age!

   - How many AMENS did I hear?

   e. James is therefore asking if anyone is sick among the body of Christ that is made up of called out believers who assemble faithfully to worship and serve God.

    3   The elders of the church to which God added the sick one are its pastors.

        a. Contrary to popular belief these early churches were very large ones: Acts 2:41 lists three thousand saved, and Acts 4:4 lists five thousand saved.

            1.) There was only one denomination of believers in town at that time, in all probability.

            2.) There was probably only one church in town at that time, but maybe many house churches.

        b. Large churches would have several pastors like the one in Acts 20:17.

        c. The term elder is used to describe the maturity that should exist in the pastoral office while the term bishop is used to identify his position in relation to others in the church, and the term pastor is used to show the relationship that should exist between the elder and his people.

        d. The elders are to minister to those who are sick—that is the reason this pastor makes hospital calling and nursing home calling two of the priorities of his ministry!

B. He Should Call The Elders Of The Church To Which The Lord Has Added Him.

    1. Notice that the sick one is to call the elders to his side (προσκαλεσάσθε).

        a. The sick one is not to try to make it to church, or to the healing service—the elders are to go to the side of the sick one or his bedside.

        b. This was not to be a public gathering, but a private encounter between the sick one, and the elders of the church to which the Lord had added him.

        c. Nowhere do we see anything about an offering being taken, or of the sick one giving a gift to the elders.

d. Please remember that James is instructing the twelve tribes scattered abroad concerning how a sick person is to respond to sickness—it is not only a local practice, but a wide spread one.
   e. This must be God's approved method of responding to sickness otherwise He would not have had James tell us about it.
2. The elders of the church to which God had added the sick one are to be called.
   a. I do not read anywhere about using someone else's hotline, ordering a anointed cloth, or writing for a prayer mat.
   b. He is to call for the elders of the church to which God added him at salvation because he is a part of that Body of Christ.
      1.) The words, let him call, certainly lay the responsibility to call upon the sick one.
      2.) He is not to place that responsibility upon someone else that may or may not call for the elders.
      3.) So often, the elders in the church hear of someone being sick via the grapevine rather than directly from the sick one, or someone in his family.
      4.) And often the elders are blamed for not coming to the side of the sick one, even though, the sick one never let the elders know that he was sick, or whether he was in the hospital or in his home.
   c. The above is God's method of dealing with sickness which has taken away the strength of the ill one—it is Scriptural, it is beneficial, and it is the best way.

II. WHAT ARE THE ELDERS OF THE CHURCH TO WHICH THE SICK ONE BELONGS TO DO FOR HIM?

A. These Elders Are To Deal With The Cause Of His Sickness.

1. They were not to go to the side of the sick one to treat him, but to help him determine the cause of his sickness.

2. Now we have already learned that sickness comes for one of three reasons:

   a. The natural consequences of the dying process taking place in us because we all have sinned, and come short of the glory of God.

      1.) It may be God's will for the sick one to be healed.

      2.) It may be God's will to use doctors, medicine, and the hospital facilities to heal the sick one.

      3.) It may be God's will to allow sin to take its toll through sickness and then allow death to occur.

      4.) Prayer will reveal that to the sick one, and to the elders who are praying for him.

   b. If the sickness is to be for God's glory then prayer will reveal that to the elders, and will give grace so the sick one to bear it.

   c. If the sickness is due to the chastening hand of the Lord being upon the sick one prayer will reveal it to both parties so that it can be dealt with Biblically.

      1.) If the sick one has committed (πεποιηκώσ-masc/part/perf/act) sins ('αμαρτίας), and the consequences of those sins are still upon him he must Biblically deal with them immediately.

      2.) This means that he must confess (to say the same thing about his sins that God says about them) those sins before any healing can take place.

         - Although this is not mentioned in particular here it is an absolute necessity according to I John 1:9.

- Therefore we must include this truth here.

- Have you ever witnessed a modern day faith healer deal with sin in a person's life before he "healed" him?

- Don't you think that he should?

- Why wouldn't he do it? Doesn't he know the Scripture? Is he ignoring the Scripture? How spiritual is he if he doesn't follow the teaching of the Word of God? Could any healing take place if the guilty person doesn't confess his sin/sins?

    3.) When confession is made, then forgiveness ('αφεθήσεται) is received, and cleansing takes place which is followed by healing.

B. These Elders Are To Anoint Him With Oil In The Name Of The Lord.

1. Let us first deal with the concept of anointing with oil ('αλείψαντεσ 'ελαίω).

   a. In secular Greek history it is used in the following ways:

      1.) To anoint the skin with oil after a bath, no healing qualities in this practice.

      2.) To anoint oneself before engaging in gymnastic exercises, no healing qualities here either.

      3.) To anoint the sick with oil, healing qualities or common comfort here, we are not sure.

   b. In Biblical history it is used in the following ways:

      1.) To anoint the head or feet with oil or ointment, Matthew 6:17; Luke 7:38.

      2.) To anoint the body for burial, Mark 16:1.

      3.) And to anoint the sick, Mark 6:13.

         In conclusion: we find that the word James uses simply means to put oil on the body for comfort purposes, especially in behalf of the sick one, and perhaps for those who have gathered to minister to the sick one, especially if some sweet smelling aroma has been added.

    c. But we do believe that this act represented the ministry of the Holy Spirit in some fashion.

2. We are now ready to consider that they are to do this in the name of the Lord.

    a. This simply means that they are doing it for the Lord or as unto the Lord, and acknowledging Him as the Healer!

    b. Notice the example of this type of ministering in Matt. 25:34-40.

    c. Now the dealing with sin, and the anointing with oil both are to take place before the prayer of faith is prayed.

        1.) You cannot pray the prayer of faith until you know what the will of the Lord is.

        2.) And James uses an aorist participle to show that the anointing preceded the praying.

C. These Elders Are To Pray Over The Sick One.

1. Now the elders are ready to do some real praying as it relates to the sick one who has called them to his side.

2. They have dealt with the cause of his sickness, he has confessed his sin, and they have anointed him with oil.

3. Let's see what happens when this procedure is followed.

III. WHAT SHALL BE THE RESULTS OF THE ELDERS' PRAYER OF FAITH?

A. The Prayer Of Faith Shall Save The Sick One.

1. Let us first of all make sure we know who is praying—it is the elders of the church to which the sick one belongs.

    a. We see, in verse fourteen, that they are to pray (προευξάσθωσαν-3p/pl/aro.1/imper) for the sick one.

b. And in verse fifteen we see that it is to be their prayer of faith that is to be prayed.

c. The elders of the church to which this man belongs are to do the praying for him.

2. Let us therefore zero in on the type of praying they are to be doing—it is to be faith praying.

a. We know that faith is always based upon the revealed will of God whether that will be revealed through the Word or through the Spirit.

b. Thus the prayer of faith is always based upon the will of God for the sick one.

c. The elders must wrestle with God until they discern the will of God for the sick one.

d. Then they can pray for the sick one properly, and every prayer of faith will cause the sick one to be healed whether he is sick of natural causes, willful sin, or for the glory of God.

1.) Nothing is mentioned about the sick man's faith being a determining factor as to whether the prayer of the elders is answered or not.

2.) However, the sick one must have had some kind of faith for he called the elders to his side to pray for him.

3.) But it is the elders' praying and faith that are on the line—not the sick ones praying and faith.

3. Let us conclude with God's assurance that this type of praying saves (σώσει-rescues, or preserves safe) the sick one every time.

B. The Lord Shall Raise Up The Sick One Over Whom The Elders Have Prayed The Prayer Of Faith.

1. As soon as the prayer of faith has been prayed God will raise up the sick one (κάμνοντα-exhausted one, one who labors under sickness).

2. Notice how this word is used in Scripture: John 2:19, Acts 3:15, Romans 4:24.

C. And If He Has Committed Sins So That The Penalty Of His Committed Sins Are Still Upon Him He Shall Be Forgiven When Sincere Confession Is Made.

1. In the case where the chastening hand of the Lord has been upon the sick one not only will his sins be forgiven him, but his sickness will be healed also.
2. You see, when he sinned, he sinned against God, and the Body of Christ to which he belongs; therefore he needs to confess his sin to God, make it right with his church, and his fellowman against whom he sinned.
   a. How many faith healers teach this Biblical truth to those they purport to have healed?
   b. Don't you think that this should be done since the whole church has been hurt by his sinful actions?
3. The elders in this case have come, they have dealt with his sin problem, and he has confessed his sin so that he could be forgiven and healed.

D. Some Final Review Thoughts.

1. If you become sick to the point that it has exhausted you, then call for the elders of he church to which you belong.
2. The elders or elder of the church will come to pray for you.
3. They/he will probably not anoint you with oil since the true significance has been lost with the passing of time.
4. But they/he will go over all this material in summary form so that they/he can pray the prayer of faith.
5. James has given us all we need to do it God's way!

Scripture Text: James 5:16.

Theme: A More Excellent Way.

Title: Divine Healing Studied, Mutual Healing Sought, IV-h.

Introduction: In this lesson we come to another one of those simple verses in James five. We have struggled through James 5:14, 15 which dealt with divine healing, and I really rejoice that James has given me some simple material to deal with in this lesson. And indeed James does make a simple statement in verse sixteen. But oh, how very difficult it is to put it into practice. Now, why would this be so? Because it gets right down to where we live, and speaks to the inner man in such a definite way that we are convicted as soon as we begin to understand what James is saying to us. Listen very carefully to him for he is giving us some sound Biblical advice that will benefit us greatly if it is followed.

I. THROUGH THE CONFESSION OF OUR FAULTS ONE TO ANOTHER.

    A. What Are We To Confess One To Another? We are to confess our faults or our offenses.

        1. The word, translated faults (παραπτώματα) is better expressed through the word offenses or the word trespasses.

        2. Thus James is talking about a situation where one believer offends another believer through a sinful act.

        3. All of the following ideas are contained in the word translated faults: to fall, to stumble aside, to take a false step, to trespass, or to offend.

        4. The common thread which runs through all of these definitions seems to speak of one brother who offends another brother through one or more of the weaknesses his fleshly nature has, thus our translation faults—that is sinful faults!

        5. This concept seems to have its roots in the trespass sin listed in the Old Testament where we read of a willful trespass, and a trespass of ignorance, Leviticus 6:1-7.

a. The willful trespass is called sin, Leviticus 5:1-6.
   b. And so is the trespass of ignorance, Leviticus 5:17-19. Did you make a mental note of this truth?
   c. Therefore when we are confessing our faults in James 5:16 we are confessing our offensive sins.
      1.) The offenders have broken the law of God.
      2.) The offenders have offended the God of the law.
      3.) The offenders have trespassed against the offended brother or sister.
B. What Does It Mean To Confess Our Offenses One To Another?
   1. To confess a sin we must say the same thing about it that God does.
      a. If God calls our faults or offenses sin, then we must also call them sin, and be convinced in our hearts that they are sins.
      b. A quick study of God's Word will help us determine whether our so-called faults are sins or not.
      c. If the Bible identifies our faults as sin we must confess them as sin!
   2. And to confess we must say the same thing about our faults as God does, and that OPENLY!
      a. If our faults were privately expressed against a brother or sister, then we must openly acknowledge our sins to the offended party.
      b. But if our faults were publicly expressed against a brother or sister then we must publicly confess them as sin before all those who were involved in the offense.
         1.) But you say, "preacher, you've got to be kidding me!"
         2.) And I reply, "God doesn't kid around in serious matters like this."

C. Why Should We Confess Our Offenses One To Another?
1. It is commanded by God through James (παραπτώματα-2p/pl/pres/imp/mid).
2. This is not an option—it is an obligation!
3. And if we do not do it we add disobedience unto our sins of offense.
4. Please notice what God thinks about disobedience, I Samuel 15:22-24.
   a. Rebellion is equal to witchcraft for it denies the true Spirit's ministry, and seeks another spirit's advice.
   b. Stubbornness is like iniquity because it is empty of any true reason to resist the directive will of God.
   c. And stubbornness is also like idolatry for it sets self on the throne of our lives instead of God.
5. Dear people of god, we cannot afford to ignore this command of God.

D. To Whom Are We To Confess Our Offenses? The offended party.
1. The guilty party is to confess his offenses to the offended party or parties.
2. This of course, presupposes that he has already confessed them to God, I John 1:9.
3. But just confessing them to God does not get the job done, he must confess them also to the offended brother in front of all those who were involved in his offenses against his brother, and then ask the offended one/ones to forgive him.
4. Some examples cited:
   a. I sinned when I told that lie about you.
   b. I sinned when I started that false rumor about you because I was envious of you.
   c. I sinned when I spoke too harshly about you, or to you.
   d. I sinned when I sought to injury you.

e. I sinned when I became jealous of you.
   5. I think we get the idea now, right?
   6. And of course, each confession must be followed by a request to be forgiven.

II. THROUGH INTERCESSOR PRAYER OFFERED ONE FOR ANOTHER.
   A. One For Another Of The Same Kind—believer praying for another believer.
      1. A non-believer could not pray for a believer for God would not hear his prayer.
      2. It is the offended believer who prays for the offending believer.
      3. This process is not to be used except where both parties are believers.
      4. We are to confess an offense against any person to that person whether he is a believer or not, but the praying one for another is believer for believer.
   B. It Is To Be The Innocent One Praying For The Guilty One.
      1. Yes, I realize that no one is entirely innocent, but it refers to the innocent one as it relates to this particular situation.
      2. It is the duty of the guilty party to confess his offense to the offended party, and before all involved in his offense whether they were participants or casual observers.
      3. It is the duty of the offended party to pray for the offender when confession has been made.
      4. Neither party may shirk his duty and remain guiltless.
      5. Now God gives us a classic example of this procedure in Job 42:7-9, *"and it was so, that after the Lord had spoken these words unto Job, the Lord said to Eliphaz, the Temanite, My wrath is kindled against thee, and against thy two friends:*

for ye have not spoken of me the thing that is right, as my servant Job hath. Therefore take unto you now seven bullocks and seven rams, and go to my servant Job, and offer up for yourselves a burnt offering; and my servant Job shall pray for you: for him will I accept: lest I deal with you after your folly, in that ye have not spoken of me the thing which is right, like my servant Job. So Eliphaz the Temanite and Bildad the Shuhite and Zophar the Naamathite went, and did according as the Lord commanded them: the Lord also accepted Job."

    a. In verses seven and eight Eliphaz, Bildad, and Zophar are commanded to confess their faults to Job for they had spoken too harshly and too severely about him.

    b. They were to take care of their sin against God by offering a burnt sacrifice.

    c. They were told that they would not be heard unless they sacrificed and confessed to Job.

    d. Then Job prayed for them, and God heard Job's prayer for them.

6. I sincerely believe that your prayers will not be heard until you follow this procedure.

7. But you say, what if the offended party will not pray for me—then you are guiltless and forgiven.

III. THROUGH PROPER CONCERN FOR THE WHOLE BODY OF CHRIST.

  A. Each Individual Is A Part Of The Whole Body Of Christ.

    1. Our text says, that ye may be healed (ἰαθῆτε).

    2. Once the confession has been made, and the prayer has been prayed the healing process can begin.

    3. That healing would be a spiritual healing in that the offense has been forgiven, and it would be a personal healing in that any consequence of the sin would be lifted according to God's will.

4. Thus the individual who had sinned would be restored to fellowship with his brother, and with the Body of Christ from which his sin severed him.

B. And These Individuals Are Part Of The Whole Body Of Christ Which Has Been Hurting Due To The Offender's Offense, I Corinthians 12:26.

1. The Body of Christ has been suffering all the time the offenses have continued without forgiveness.

2. It would be like perhaps, an earache, in an otherwise healthy body making the whole body suffer.

3. It could however have a much greater effect on the body like a stroke, or a heart attack that incapacitates the whole body.

4. Then the whole body would suffer greatly.

5. In light of this awesome potential James tells us to confess our faults one to another, and pray one for another that we may be healed.

6. The offense relates to two or perhaps a few more, but the whole body suffers because of it.

7. Do you see now why we must practice this great Scriptural truth?

   a. Do you need to do some confessing?

   b. It will not be easy for you to do it!

   c. But your prayers will not be heard, and the Body of Christ will suffer, maybe, greatly until you do.

Scripture Text: II Kings 5:11.

Theme: A More Excellent Way.

Title: Divine Healing Studied, Three Fallacies About It, IV-i.

Introduction: With all the renewed emphasis upon divine healing today I thought it would be appropriate to address this topic as my closing lesson on this subject. However as I write on the subject I want to look at it through the eyes of the non-Christian, and the non-spiritual person so that we can understand why so many unbelievers, and so many fleshly believers are so easily led astray in this area. We shall find our examples in Naaman and Gehazi. Naaman was a non-believing leper seeking divine healing, and Gehazi was a non-spiritual man seeking to profit from divine healing. Between them they had three false concepts about divine healing, the first being:

I. IT CAN BE SECURED BY THE WILL OF MAN.

   A. The Condition Of Naaman, II Kings 5:1.

      1. To the casual observer he had all that life could offer to him.

         a. For he was captain of the host of Syria when Syria was a great power.

         b. For he was a great man with his Master, the king.

         c. For he was an honorable man in the eyes of the people of Syria.

         d. For he had been used (knowingly or unknowingly) by the Lord to deliver Syria from her enemies.

         e. And he was a man of valor, but he was battling an enemy that he could not defeat.

      2. To the careful observer he was a leper.

         a. This disease was slowly debilitating him, and would soon render him useless as a soldier.

         b. This disease would soon cause him to become a social outcast although at the present he could keep it hidden from the general public.

c. And this disease would someday cause him to be separated from his wife.

d. Thus Naaman desired with all his heart to be healed, and he was willing to go to any extent to be healed.

e. He expresses the attitude that most of those who are ill have—they are desperate to be healed! They will try anything to be healed! They will pay any price to be healed! They will believe in almost anyone to be healed!

B. The Information That Came To Naaman, II Kings 5:2-4.

1. There is a prophet of God in Israel who can cure you of your leprosy.

2. The source of the information was a little captive Israelite maid.

3. She tells Naaman's wife, who tells a servant, who tells Naaman, who tells the king of Syria.

4. And the king of Syria told him to go immediately.

5. Notice some things with me:

   a. He doesn't know the prophet's name, nor where he lives, but he goes.

   b. He has heard the story from a captive maid, why should he believe her?

   c. And he'll have to make the journey into the enemy's country.

   d. But he'll go, and so would many of us so long as there was hope, strength, and the resources to go.

   e. However, as you go you had better make sure you have a Biblical understanding concerning divine healing.

C. The Actions Of Naaman, II Kings 5:5-7.

1. He leaves with a letter from his king unto the king of Israel.

   a. The letter is a request for the king of Israel to heal Naaman, or to see that he is healed by the prophet of God, II Kings 5a-6.

    b. When will mankind learn that all divine healing must be done in accordance with God's will?

    c. Faith will not heal you if it is not the will of God for you to be healed since faith is always based on the will of God, II Corinthians 12:8-10.

    d. Discern the will of God first, then pray the prayer of faith to be healed, or to receive His strength.

    e. The king of Israel's reply should remind us forever that divine healing cannot be secured by man, *"And it came to pass, when the king of Israel had read the letter, that he rent his clothes, and said, Am I God, to kill and to make alive, that this man doth send unto me to recover a man of his leprosy,"* II Kings 5:7?

2. He leaves with a large sum of money, and much clothing.

    a. Ten talents of silver would be an enormous amount of money for that time period.

    b. Six thousand pieces of gold would be many times over the amount of the silver.

    c. Ten changes of raiment or holiday suits would express extreme wealth for the average man who could not even afford one suit.

    d. But if the cure can be purchased through the will of man—Naaman is ready to pay for it!

        1.) Sad to say every religious con artist knows this, and is most happy to take all that Naaman has, and even more if he can get it.

        2.) Naaman represents all those in his predicament as it relates to what they are willing to do to be healed.

        3.) If the healing is of God, then God should receive the praise, but man should not receive the money! AMEN?

II. IT MUST BE ACCOMPANIED BY MUCH FANFARE.
  A. In That A Public Display Is Needed, II Kings 5:11a.
    1. Now when Elisha heard of the actions and words of the king of Israel he sent him word that there was a prophet of God in Israel, and that Naaman should come to him, II Kings 5:8.
       a. A prophet is a revealer of the will of God.
       b. A prophet is an interpreter of the Word of God.
       c. Thus a prophet is qualified to discern whether Naaman should be healed by God or not.
    2. However when Naaman arrived with his wealth, his company, and his leprosy Elisha didn't even go out to greet him.
       a. Man wants to be welcomed to his healing, flattered about his healing, and to be involved in his healing.
       b. But Elisha teaches us that God is the true healer, and that the true man of God remains in the background of any healing so that God can receive all the glory and praise.
       c. Would to God that every child of God took this same attitude as was displayed by Elisha.
    3. But he did send a message by his servant to Naaman, II Kings 5:10.
       a. Earthly protocol demanded that common man greet the great Syrian leader with great respect.
       b. But heavenly wisdom would teach Naaman that he was the servant of Elisha, II Kings 5:15c.
       c. However, Naaman had not learned that lesson yet, and I wonder if my generation will ever learn it.
    4. Therefore Naaman was very upset that his healing would take place in the muddy Jordan where no public fanfare would accompany it, nor would the prophet of God be there with him when he was healed, II Kings 5:12.

a. Should he be concerned about the manner in which he was healed, or should he be satisfied to be healed?

b. Should he try to dictate the terms of his healing when he couldn't heal himself, when the king of Israel could not do it either, or when no one else he knew could heal him?

c. Some are not content with God's way of healing; therefore they try to improve upon it by making a public spectacle of it, making a profit from it, and getting personal fame from it.

5. Only the intercession of his servants saved him from remaining a leper.

a. Would you do something great if he asked you? Yes! Of Course I Would! Just Name It and I'll Do It!

b. Then do something small for it may be the greatest thing you have ever done in your life!

c. And it was, II Kings 5:14!

B. In That Some Verbal Utterance Must Be Said, II kings 5:11a, *"But Naaman was wroth, and went away, and said, Behold, I thought, He will surely come out to me and stand, and call on the name of the Lord his God."*

1. God can hear the prayer of the heart much better than the prayer of the loud praise seeking mouth.

2. But the non-spiritual man expects a verbal utterance from the healer before healing can take place.

3. Elisha shows us that this concept is false, and entirely unnecessary.

a. Pre and post apostolic times used the method of Elisha because it is God's way. Would to God that every sick person would learn this!

b. Apostolic times used the verbal commands openly to establish the messenger and the message.

C. In That Some Physical Contact Must Be Made, II kings 5:11b, *"and strike his hand over the place, and recover the leper."*

1. Naaman thought Elisha must strike his hands over the leprosy before he could be healed.

2. Modern day faith healers milk this false concept to the point that they exploit all who are not wise Biblically.

3. God can and does heal without any physical contact being made by the healer. Have you notice how many so-called faith healers strike the person to be healed in one manner or another? Surely they follow this evil concept of Naaman!

III. IT SHOULD BE REWARDED WITH A MONETARY GIFT, II Kings 5:20-27.

A. Naaman's Offer.

1. Take a blessing of thy servant for I came prepared to pay for my healing, II Kings 5:15, 16a.

    a. I am certainly able to give it unto you.

    b. You are certainly in need of what I can give you.

    c. Divine healing is not to be sold on the open market like the things of this world.

    d. If you had to pay for your divine healing—it would not be divine healing.

    e. Elisha says, "as the Lord liveth before whom I stand I will receive none."

2. But Naaman urged him to take it, 5:16b.

    a. You'd better not urge a twenty first century healer to take it—he'll take it, and all that he can get besides that.

    b. In fact, he'll ask you for it, if you do not give it, or he'll chide you about cheating the Lord if you don't give it.

    c. Elisha refused to take anything at all.

B. Gehazi's Request, II Kings 5:20-24.
   1. Let us look into the heart of the non-spiritual man to see that he thinks that he deserves to be paid for God healing Naaman.
      a. As a Christian worker who has been called by God to do His work, I have the duty to instruct believers to give Scripturally. I have the right to lay any current need relating to the Lord's work before the believers, and ask them to pray about what part the Lord would have them to have in meeting that need. However, I do not have the authority from God or man to ask them to give sacrificially until I am willing to sacrifice to the same extent that I am asking them to sacrifice. Am I Right? ABSOLUTELY!
      b. Why should those who live in dire poverty and those who live "hand to mouth" support those who live in the lap of luxury, drive expensive automobiles, wear designer clothes, and eat gourmet foods? I certainly would be fearful of standing before the Righteous Judge of all flesh having fleeced the flock of God in the name of the Lord to support my inappropriate manner of living.
      c. Yes, I do know that most Christian workers would not be guilty of seeking filthy lucre, but far too many are. One is actually to many for me! How about you?
   2. He speaks for all who seek to profit from what God alone has done.
   3. Thus he asks for a talent of silver, and two changes of raiment.
   4. But Naaman gives two talents of silver and two changes of raiment.
C. Elisha's Judgment, II Kings 5:25-27.
   1. I know what you have done for my heart went with you. Could God say this of you or me?

2. Is it a time for us to seek worldly possessions when God healed Naaman? You and I had no part in it!
3. The leprosy of Naaman shall be upon you and your seed forever.
    a. When we try to sell what God has freely given we cheapen God's gift.
    b. And when we sell what He has freely given, we sin grievously against God, Acts 8:18-23.
    c. If this Old Testament example were executed upon those who sell healing today, we'd be building new leprosariums for many years to come to house them.
    d. Divine healing comes from only God, it is free, and it is for only those God wills to heal. Divine healing is not for everyone, but divine grace is for everyone who will receive it!

Scripture Text: I Corinthians 12:10, 29.

Theme: A More Excellent Way.

Title: Divine Miracles.

Introduction: Divine Miracles have been variously defined throughout Church History. This variety of definitions has often caused many misunderstandings among Bible believers. I do believe in divine miracles even for today, but do not believe in miracle workers! In one sense of the term divine miracles were only for the apostolic age. Perhaps we should refer to God's workings of today as supernatural events. True Bible miracles were sensible, supernatural, redemptive, and done through a miracle worker. The word miracle has come to mean other than that in our culture. Let us therefore study the Scriptures to see what they say.

I. MIRACLES DEFINED.

   A. Webster's Definition Of A Miracle.

      1. *"An event or effect in the physical world deviating from the known laws of nature, or transcending our knowledge of these laws."*

      2. *"A wonder or wonderful thing or a marvel."*

   B. The Biblical Definition Of A Miracle.

      1. Two words are translated miracle in the New Testament.

         a. δύναμισ is an act of power, translated miracle when found in a supernatural context.

         b. σημεῖον is a sign and is translated both sign and miracle according to the context (at least twenty-two times it is translated miracle in the New Testament).

         c. The word, δύναμισ, is used when the act in particular is referred to, and the word, σημεῖον, is used when the results of the act are in view.

      2. A Biblical miracle is an act of power or sign used to demonstrate God's presence and approval.

C. The Limitations Of Biblical Miracles.
1. They must be sensible, Acts 4:16.
   a. This miracle was observable to the eye.
   b. It was undeniable due to the witnesses.
2. They must be supernatural in nature, John 9:30-33.
   a. This man was born blind, but he was healed by Jesus.
   b. The Pharisees denied that Jesus did it by the power of God, John 9:24.
   c. But the healed man makes the following statements:
      1.) God hears not sinners, but worshippers, John 9:31.
      2.) This thing has not been heard of before in Israel, John 9:32.
      3.) If he were not of God he could not have done this miracle, John 9:33.
3. They must have a redemptive significance, John 20:30, 31, *"And many other signs truly did Jesus in the presence of his disciples, which are not written in this book: But these are written, that ye might believe that Jesus is the Christ, the Son of God; and that believing ye might have life through his name."*
   a. Signs were given that ye may believe.
   b. Miracles were not performed just for the asking.
   c. They had a definite purpose—redemption of the lost.
4. They must be performed by an agent of God.
   a. All of the Biblical miracles were performed by men of God.
   b. These signs authenticated their message.
   c. Even Jesus was authenticated by signs, Acts 2:22, *"Ye men of Israel, hear these words; Jesus of Nazareth, a man approved of God among you by miracles and wonders*

and signs, which God did by him in the midst of you, as ye yourselves also know."

II. THE PURPOSE OF DIVINE MIRACLES.

A. To Authenticate The Person Of Christ, His Words, His Work, And His Workers.

1. His person, John 20:30, 31.

    a. Jesus told the people of His day that they would not believe except they saw signs and wonders, John 4:48.

    b. Luke tells us that Jesus was a man approved among the people of his day by signs and wonders, Acts 2:22.

    c. In John 2:11 we learn that the miracles of Jesus began at the wedding of Cana of Galilee.

    d. Others believed when they saw His miracles, John 2:23.

        1.) John 6:14 tells us that some concluded that Jesus was that prophet when they saw His miracles.

        2.) Some others asked, will Messiah do more miracles than this man, John 7:31?

    e. Jesus said that His works proved that He was the Messiah.

        1.) And that the Father had sent Him, John 5:36.

        2.) Nothing more was needed to believe, John 10:24, 25.

        3.) If you are in doubt, then observe Him as He worked, Luke 7:20-22.

2. His words.

    a. The Old Testament Scriptures were confirmed by angels, but the New Testament was confirmed by signs and wonders, Hebrews 2:2-4.

    b. New Testament preachers had their word confirmed by miracles, Mark 16:20.

3. His workers.
   a. Stephen, Acts 6:8.
   b. Philip, Acts 8:6, 13.
   c. Paul, Romans 15:19.

B. To Attempt To Authenticate The Antichrist And His False Words.
   1. Of course we know that these are false signs and wonders.
   2. Yet in the Tribulational Period miracles will abound again as the antichrist seeks to authenticate his ministry.
      a. This was predicted by Jesus, Mark 13:22, 23.
         1.) Beloved beware of anyone who seeks to authenticate his ministry by the miracles he performs.
         2.) Christ's ministry has already been authenticated, but the antichrist's ministry hasn't.
      b. II Thessalonians 2:9 tells us that antichrist will come with all power, signs, and lying wonders.
      c. Revelation 13:14 tells us that he will deceive those who dwell on the earth by his miracles.
      d. Revelation 16:14 says that the spirit of demons works miracles to cause men to war against the Almighty.
         1.) But you say, is this possible?
         2.) Listen to what Jesus says in John 5:43, *"I am come in my Father's name, and ye receive me not: if another shall come in his own name, him ye will receive."*
      e. Revelation 19:20 states the end of the false prophet who did miracles for the antichrist.
   3. Beloved, make sure you know what you are doing when you fellow a miracle worker!
   4. Jesus you know, but others---be sure you try them.
   5. I believe we are being set-up for the revelation of the antichrist with all this renewed emphasis on miracles.

III. THE SCOPE OF THE MIRACLES WAS UNLIMITED.
   A. The dead were raised, John 11:43, 44.
   B. The maimed were made whole, Matthew 15:30a.
   C. The blind were able to see, Matthew 15:30b.
   D. The dumb were made to speak, Matthew 15:30c.
   E. The lame were made to walk, Matthew 15:30d.
   F. The sick were healed, Matthew 15:30e.
   G. The elements were controlled, Matthew 8:26, 27.

IV. THE DURATION OF THE MIRACLES WAS FIXED.
   A. Not By Man, But By God Until His Messengers' Messages Were Inscripturated.
   B. Once This Was Accomplished The Witness Of The Holy Spirit To The Word Of God He Had Authored Was So Much Better Than Signs And Works Of Power That They Ceased.
      1. You have a much more reliable witness in the Holy Spirit, and the Word He authored than in signs and miracles, II Peter 1:19-21.
      2. This is true because the antichrist will use lying signs and wonders to fool you, II Thessalonians 2:9.
   C. Seek After Only Those Things That Can Be Borne Witness To By The Holy Spirit.
      1. He will never contradict the Word of God.
      2. He will never promote Himself, but He will lift up Jesus Christ, John 15:26, 16:13, 14.
      3. He will never give any more revelation—He now only ILLUMINATES THE UNDERSTANDING OF BELIEVERS RELATING TO WHAT HE HAS ALREADY REVEALED!

V. DO WE NEED DIVINE MIRACLES TODAY?

- A. No, Because They Do Not Guarantee Belief.
    1. In John 6:26 many witnessed the miracles, but did not believe.
    2. In John 9:16 the miracle caused a division to develop.
    3. In John 12:37 even though they saw many miracles they did not believe.
- B. No, Because A Wicked Generation Seeketh A Sign.
    1. Matthew 12:38, 39, states that an evil and adulterous generation seeketh a sign.
    2. In Mark 8:11, we see the Pharisees seeking a sign from heaven.
    3. Jesus did not give it, but antichrist will do it for those who ask it of him, Revelation 13:11-14.
- C. No, Because We Have All We Need To Believe.
    1. Abraham told the rich man that he had Moses and the prophets to believe, Luke 16:29.
    2. Abraham says a miracle would not cause the rich man's five brothers to believe if they had already rejected the message of the Old Testament, Luke 16:31.
    3. If we deny the New Testament Scriptures we would not believe even if a man returned from the dead.
- D. No, Because Preaching Produces Believers, I Corinthians 1:21.
    1. The Jews require a sign and the Greeks seek wisdom, but Paul preached Christ unto them, I Corinthians 1:22.
    2. If the message reaches not the world, neither will miracles.
    3. Why seek a sign when you can have the real thing, I Corinthians 15:22.

E. No, Because My Experience Tells Me That I Did Not Need Them.
   1. I was a sinner lost for all of eternity.
   2. I didn't witness a miracle, but I did hear the Word of God that touched my heart.
   3. And I believed with all of my heart unto salvation.
   4. I doubt that anyone reading this book was converted through a true Biblical miracle, except the miracle of SALVATION!
   5. WE HAVE ALL THAT WE NEED FOR WE HAVE THE WORD, THE SPIRIT, AND THE SAVIOR!

F. No, Because It Is Better To Believe Without A Miracle, Than to Believe Because Of A Miracle, John 20:29.
   1. Jesus tells Thomas he believed only because of the miracle of the resurrection.
   2. But He says, blessed are those who believe and have not seen My hands and My side.
      a. Stability in Christ causes us to rely on Jesus, not on emotion or miracles.
      b. Seeking miracles shows a real lack of faith in God's Word.
      c. Faith is increased by hearing the Word, not seeing miracles, Romans 10:17.
      d. God still performs His wonders to behold, but He does not use a miracle worker to do them.

G. No, But God Can Still Perform A Miracle Anytime He Chooses.
   1. He does not need me or you or anyone else.
   2. Let us let God be God for only then will He be able to meet the needs of our heart!

Scripture Text: I Corinthians 12:10.

Theme: A More Excellent Way.

Title: Divine Prophecy.

Introduction: Divine Prophecy is one of the most thrilling studies found in the Word of God. The whole prophetical movement is amazing in scope. I believe in divine prophecy, study it frequently, and preach on it often. I also believe in divine prophets, but do not feel that they are needed today since redemption's story is now complete. Neither do I feel any so-called prophet could meet the test God says we are to use to test a prophet. However, according to Scripture many false prophets shall arise, and we are warned to test them. God also condemns all forms of seeking the future outside the realm of divine prophecy. Notice then what the Scriptures teach.

I. THE TEST FOR A DIVINE PROPHET, DEUTERONOMY 18:22.

   A. He Must Speak In The Name Of The Lord.

      1. The prophets of the Scripture said: Thus Saith The Lord, or THE LORD SAID.

      2. They assumed the responsibility for using the Lord's Name to authenticate their words.

      3. Hear what God says about using His name in vain, Exodus 20:7.

   B. What He Says Must Come To Pass Each Time He Speaks In The Name Of The Lord.

      1. God says that if he isn't always right, then he is not a prophet of God.

      2. He cannot be 50% right, 75% right, or even 90% right, but he must be 100% right every time he speaks to qualify as a prophet of God.

      3. We are NOT to hear him at all if his words are false, neither are we to receive him, or help him in any way, II John 1:7-11, *"For many deceivers are entered into the world, who confess not that Jesus Christ is come in the flesh. This is a*

deceiver and an antichrist. Look to yourselves, that we lose not those things which we have wrought, but that we receive a full reward. Whosoever transgresseth, and abideth not in the doctrine of Christ, hath not God. He that abideth in the doctrine of Christ, he hath both the Father and the Son. If there come any unto you, and bring not this doctrine, receive him not into your house, neither bid him God speed: For he that biddeth him God speed is partaker of his evil deeds."

    4. I have yet to meet the man who can pass this test!

  C. His Message Must Be Revelational, Not Interpretational.

    1. So many so-called prophets simply take a prophecy found in the Word, and predict that it will come true—that is not prophesying as it pertains to the foretelling ministry of the prophet.

    2. True prophecy will contain new revelation.

    3. Many people know so little about the Bible that they do not know new prophecy from old prophecy.

    4. True prophecy is not based on the predictable future—it reveals the unforeseeable future.

  D. Conclusions:

    1. I have never met the man who has passed the test that God has left us to discern whether a man is a prophet or fraud.

    2. Until I do I will not accept the lies of the false prophets who not only try to deceive those who listen to them, but deceive even themselves in the process.

II. THE SCRIPTURAL PURPOSE OF PROPHECY.

  A. To Instruct In A Redemptive Context.

    1. All the prophetical utterances that did not deal with the future showed what would happen to those who were disobedient unto God and/or His Word.

      a. This is the forth-telling ministry of the prophet of God.

      b. He did this through Holy men who were carried along by the Holy Spirit of God, II Peter 1:19, 20.

      c. This forth-telling ministry will continue to proclaim the message the prophets gave to us through their preaching and writing, I Corinthians 15:4.

      d. Their message was primarily to God's people as it relates to their forth-telling ministry.

  2. The main message to Israel was that captivity was coming if she did not repent.

  3. Deuteronomy 29:29b says, *but those things revealed belong unto us and to our children for ever, that we may do all the words of the law."*

B. To Predict Redemptive Future.

  1. This is the foretelling ministry of the prophets.

  2. It sets forth what the future holds as it relates to sacred history in the future.

  3. The central message of the prophets was Jesus Christ, John 1:45.

  4. From Moses (Acts 3:22) to Samuel, and from Samuel to Christ all the prophets spoke of His coming, Acts 3:24.

  5. They emphasized salvation through Christ, Acts 10:43.

  6. All of the Old Testament prophets spoke of His coming, or prepared us for His coming.

  7. All of the New Testament prophets spoke of His coming or prepared us for His second coming.

  8. God has laid out the complete future for us in His Word as it pertains to all we need—all we have to do is study it, understand it, and apply it!

  9. Revelation 19:10 says that the spirit of prophecy is testifying about Jesus.

C. To Provide A Reliable Record Until The Canon Was Complete.
  1. God used Spirit led men to provide this record.
     a. For Holy men spoke in time past as they were carried along by the Holy Spirit, II Peter 1:19, 20.
     b. But in the last days God spoke through His Son, Jesus, Hebrews 1:2a.
     c. And Paul speaks in the Church Age to the church saints telling them that the foretelling ministry of the prophets shall be done away with by God when the Bible is complete—it has now been complete for centuries.
        1.) There is no need to seek further revelation through the foretelling ministry of the prophets for none shall be forthcoming.
        2.) The passive voice of the verb (καταργηθ²σονται) tells us that an outside force (God) shall cause prophecies to be done away with, that is, when the Bible is completed. As of this writing Paul says that it was not complete, but we conclude that it was completed by the end of the first century.
        3.) We have every prophecy that we need, both now and forever, and they are found only in the Bible!
        4.) The prophets were involved in a foretelling ministry and a forth-telling ministry, thus they sought to help us understand both aspects of their ministry. That's what our ministry is to be today—nothing more, nothing less.
  2. Two more prophets shall arise in the future, but they shall not minister during the Church Age. Their ministry will be during the Great Tribulation, Revelation 11:3-10.
  3. However, you must be warned that many false prophets shall arise and abound, Matthew 24:11, I John 4:1.

III. WHAT DOES THE BIBLE SAY ABOUT SEEKING THE FUTURE?

   A. The Secret Things Belong To The Lord, Deuteronomy 29:29.

      1. Satan wanted to be like God and fell, so did Eve.

      2. God is not obligated to reveal our personal future to us—we are to trust and obey! Really, there is no other way!

      3. Our walk is by faith in His revealed Word, not by sight.

      4. Satan will deceive many who try to find out the secrets of God.

   B. God Reveals All Man Needs To Know.

      1. He does withhold facts about people, events, and places lest we begin to play God.

      2. Satan told Eve that she would be like God if she disobeyed God.

      3. God will not withhold any good things from us, Psalm 84:11.

   C. All Other Means Of Revelation Seeking Are Condemned.

      1. The false means identified. All definitions full or in part under this heading are taken from *ZONDERVAN'S PICTORAL BIBLE DICTIONARY.*

         a. Astrology is the practice of conjuring or dividing the heavens to discern the future.

            1.) To conjure means to summons a demon by an incantation, Daniel 2:5-10.

            2.) To divide the heavens means to assign certain fates to certain signs, Isaiah 47:13.

         b. Divination means to determine the future by use of trances, drugs, and/or visions.

            1.) Acts 16:16 tells us that the young lady had a spirit of divination.

            2.) Paul cast the spirit out of her—she was demon possessed.

3.) This is an evil practice of Satan, never use it.

c. Enchantment, sorcery, or witchcraft means to whisper a magic spell.

1.) Acts 8:10, 11 says that Simon the sorcerer had bewitched them with sorcery, and that they considered him to be a great man of God. Multitudes are still doing this today! How wicked this is, and how sad it is!

2.) Acts 13:6-11 says that Barjesus the sorcerer tried to hinder the Gospel message from being preached by Paul.

3.) Some people actually believed that these evil men were from God, Act 8:10. Can YOU believe this?

d. Familiar spirits speak of those who act as a medium to seek the spirit world.

1.) Saul sought such a person, I Samuel 28:8.

2.) I Chronicles 10:13, 14 says that Saul died for this act and others.

3.) God wants us to speak to the ever-living Lord God Almighy, not the physically dead!

e. Necromancy is the practice of seeking the dead.

1.) Sin separated Saul from God, but instead of confessing his sin, he sought the dead.

2.) Satan makes us think we can know the future through these sinful means.

f. Observer of times, and the soothsayer both mean to cloud over the issue.

1.) They make it so cloudy that you believe the lie to the point that you are found practicing the lie.

2.) Satan is a lair from the beginning and is the father of it.

3.) God has given the times and the seasons to know the present, not the future.

g. The word wizard comes from a word meaning to know.

   1.) Those who know things about you without knowing you first fit into this class.

   2.) They are empowered by Satan, never God.

   3.) Fortune-tellers, and all such like should be shunned like the plague.

2. The false means studied:

   a. They cannot know the future, Daniel 2:8, 9, 27, 28.

   b. Mediums and wizards peep and mutter, Isaiah 8:19.

   c. Seeking these will defile you, Leviticus 19:31.

   d. When you seek them you play the harlot with God, Leviticus 20:6.

   e. Those who practice these evils seldom repent, Revelation 9:21.

   f. Their practice is to deceive, Revelation 18:23.

   g. Their end is perdition, Revelation 21:8.

   h. They shall not see heaven, Revelation 22:15.

3. The false means condemned.

   a. Deuteronomy 18:19-22.

      1.) We are commanded not to learn their ways, Deuteronomy 18:9.

      2.) God judges those who practice these things, Deuteronomy 18:12.

   b. Leviticus 20:27.

      1.) These practices were worthy of death.

      2.) Saul had killed most of them, I Samuel 28:9.

      3.) Saul died for two reasons: not obeying the Word of God, and for seeking counsel from one having a familiar spirit, I Chronicles 10:13, 14.

IV. WHAT SHOULD BE OUR ATTITUDE TOWARDS PROHECY?
   A. Shun All That God Shuns.
      1. Don't get involved in it, don't study it, don't practice it—don't even read too much about it.
      2. Satan may get a hold on you that you cannot break.
      3. Believe the Word, not false prophets.
      4. God speaks only through divine prophets.
      5. A prophet must meet the test of a prophet before we accept him.
   B. Study The Prophecies In The Word Of God To Know The Future.
      1. God has it all outlined for you.
      2. He hasn't left out a single thing you NEED to know.
      3. The Bible is rich in prophecy just waiting for you to study it, profit from it, and share it with the uninformed.
      4. Yes, I know that this would be the hard way, but it is the only right way!
      5. Acknowledge God in all your ways, and He shall direct your path. Believe the Scriptures for they shall judge you in the end, John 12:48.
   C. Compare Prophesying To Tongue Speaking, I Corinthians 14:1-4.
      1. It is better than desiring other spiritual gifts.
      2. It is better because there is more understanding,
      3. It is better because it edifies, exhorts, and comforts the common man, 3.
      4. It is better because it edifies the church, 4, 5.
      5. It is better to speak only five words by prophesying than to speak ten thousand words by an unknown tongue, 19.

Scripture Text: I Corinthians 12:10.

Theme: A More Excellent Way.

Title: Discerning of Spirits, VII.

Introduction: This is one of those easier passages that we have to deal with in our study of the so-called charismatic gifts. Nevertheless it is one of those passages that we really need to get hold of and let it get hold of us. I say this because we truly need to have discernment in these days in which we now find ourselves. What would it be like if we did not have the Bible to guide us? I would be fearful of making any decision that called for accepting or rejecting anyone else as it pertains to whether they would qualify to do this or that. With this thought on our minds let us then begin our study.

I. ITS MEANING: (διακρίσεισ πνενμάτων) having the ability to separate, make a distinction, or to distinguish one from another.

   A. Since The Early Church Did Not Have All Of The Word To Use As A Standard Of Judgment—it needed the gift of discerning of spirits.

   B. How Well Could We Judge If We Had Not The Word To Use As Our Standard Of Judgment?

   C. But God Blessed The Early Church With This Gift, And He Has Blessed Us With Our Completed Bible!

II. ITS PURPOSE: to keep believers from error as it relates to religious decisions that needed to be made.

   A. If We Have All The Trouble That We Now Have Discerning Between Those Who Are True, And Those Who Are False, Just Think What A Job The Early Church Must Have Had!

   B. Then Realize How Good God Was To Give The Gift Of Discerning Of Spirits To Some—NOT ALL, BUT SOME!

   C. Not All Received This Gift—Only Those The Holy Spirit Chose As He Willed.

III. ITS DURATION: it would last until the written Word could give us all the information we needed to make a proper decision as to whether a person was of God or the devil, and whether written material was inspired by God or man.

    A. We Must Work Under The Supervision Of The Holy Spirit In This Present Time.

    B. But Now We All Have Access To The Word, And The Holy Spirit At All Times.

    C. I Praise God For This: I Trust That You Do Also!

IV. ITS NECESSITY.

    A. Because There Were Many Deceivers In Their World, II John 1:7-11.

        1. They faced false brethren who would use whatever means they had available to them to deceive whomsoever they could, II Corinthians 11:26, Galatians 2:4.

        2. They faced false teachers who would teach them false doctrines, II Peter 2:1.

        3. They faced false prophets who would lead them astray, I John 4:1-3.

        4. They faced false christs who would tell them that they were the Promised Messiah, Matthew 24:24.

        5. They faced false apostles who tried to use their position to take advantage of believers, II Corinthians 11:13.

    B. Because Their Adversaries Were Stronger And Wiser Than They Were.

        1. I Peter 5:8 gives us a vivid picture of the type of individual they faced, *"Be sober, be vigilant; because your adversary the devil, as a roaring lion, walketh about seeking whom he may devour."*

        2. II Corinthians 11:13-15 tells us, *"For such are false apostles, deceitful workers, transforming themselves into apostles of*

Christ. And no marvel, for Satan himself is transformed into an angel of light. Therefore it is no great thing if his ministers also be transformed as the ministers of righteousness; whose end shall be according to their works."

3. And Matthew 24:24 tells us that if it were not for the intercession of God Satan would deceive even the elect, *"For there shall arise false Christs, and false prophets, and shall show great signs and wonders; insomuch that, if it were possible, they shall deceive the very elect."*

C. Because Without The Whole Bible They Could Not Judge As We Are Now Commanded To Do.

1. By their fruits they could know them, Matthew 7:16-20.
2. They also could try every spirit, I John 4:1-3.
3. But now we can use every standard found in the Word of God.

    1.) The Word enlightens, the Spirit convicts.
    2.) The Word gives the Holy Spirit the ammunition He needs to blow away every false doctrine!
    3.) They had common sense, the Spirit, and the gift.
    4.) We have common sense, the Spirit, and the eternal Word of God!

V. ITS WARNINGS:

A. Don't Listen To A Single False Prophet!
B. Don't Accept Any Teaching From Any False Prophet!
C. Don't Practice Any Doctrine Of Any False Prophet!
D. Don't Promote Any Activities Of Any False Prophet!
E. Don't Allow Any False Prophet To Fellowship With You!
F. Don't Tolerate Any Overture Of Any False Prophet!
G. Don't Wish God Speed To Any False Prophet, II John 1:11.

Scripture Text: I Corinthians 12:10.

Theme: A More Excellent Way.

Title: Divers Kinds Of Tongues, VIII, a.

Introduction: As we introduce this eighth so-called charismatic gift it will be a short introductory study just to set forth three main thoughts: Its Meaning, Its Purpose, and Its Duration. I do this because I believe that the rest of the study depends upon our understanding of this material. May we then drink fully, one item at a time.

I. ITS MEANING: having the ability to speak a language that you did not know previously, and had not taken lessons to learn.

    A. The Gospel Message Needed To Be Carried Throughout The Known World Very Quickly; Therefore God Enabled Certain Ones To Convey The Gospel Message To Foreigners In Their Own Languages (γένη γλωσσῶν).

    B. Thus He Supernaturally Gave Them The Ability To Speak Known Languages That They Had Not Previously Known How To Speak.

    C. This Caused The Hearers To Listen More Intently (Acts 22:2) To What Was Being Said.

II. ITS PURPOSE: to serve as a sign to the unbeliever, I Corinthians 14:22.

    A. This Sign Gift Was Not To Be Used Among Believers, In The Church, Or For Self-Edification.

    B. It Was To Be Used To Reach The Non-believer In Every Nation Being Reached By The Missionary Efforts By Any Local Church.

    C. Why Then Do We Have Such An Over-emphasis Upon Its Usage In Some Churches Today?

    D. Are They So Desperate To Prove That They Are More Spiritual Than Anyone Else That They Have Developed A False Standard For Verifying Their So-called Spirituality?

III. ITS DURATION: the verb in I Corinthians 13:8 (παύσονται) is a middle voice verb informing us that tongues will stop, leave off, or refrain from use in and of themselves.

　A. If They Are For Today, Then Every Church That Speaks In Tongues Should Not Commission Any Missionary Who Cannot Speak The Language Of The People Of The Field He Is Going To Since It Would Be A Total Waste Of Time, Money, And Effort.

　　1. If I believed that speaking with an unknown tongue, as defined by those in the charismatic movement, were for today, then I would see to it that every person seeking to be a missionary would be subjected to every available means to me to get them directly to the mission field so they would not waste the time, the effort, and the money it takes to learn a foreign language.

　　2. Since it takes from two to three or even more years to raise their support, two to three years or even more to go to language school training to be able to speak a foreign language moderately well, and then add a year of furlough before you total up the cost in time, effort, and money.

　　　a. That's about a five-year average in time.

　　　b. And that could easily add up to $50,000.00 a year for four to seven years. I'll let you do the math!

　　3. Why not teach them to secure the gift, and put them directly to work? The reason is that it cannot be done, it is not being done, and no one has plans to do it.

　　4. When I'm on the mission field I am useless if I can't speak the language of those I am trying to minister unto. I would have to learn the language or use an interpreter in every case. Do you know of any missionary who has been divinely gifted so that he went directly to the mission field without having to learn to speak the foreign language of those he would be ministering unto?

5. If tongues are a sign unto the unbeliever, then every person who professes to be able to speak with tongues ought to spend all of his time reaching the lost. Would you say Amen to that?

B. Evidently, The Gift Is No Longer Available To Us, Especially As It Pertains To Its Primary Purpose.

C. If This Is True, And It Is, Then We Should Be Ashamed To Use It In Any Other Way! SHOULD WE NOT?

Scripture Text: I Corinthians 12:10.

Theme: A More Excellent Way.

Title: Divers Kinds Of Tongues, VIII-b, What Does It Mean To Speak In Tongues?

Introduction: As we approach the second lesson on this subject let me say that some folks have had their lives changed by becoming involved in the tongues movement. However, over the long run it has been to their detriment rather than their betterment. As I have told you before so tell I you once again—speaking in tongues is not a sign of ones spirituality, but a gift dispensed by the Holy Spirit as He wills. It is like any other gift—it can be used or abused! However, one should make special note of the fact that God lists it as the least of all gifts, I Corinthians 12:28. Why would a Spirit filled person then seek the least of all gifts? He Would Not! However, a person wanting you to think that he was filled with the Spirit would want a showy gift to impress others. Satan deceives that person into believing that he can deceive us by his gift when all he is doing is glorifying self instead of Christ. This is contrary to the teaching of the Word. No Spirit filled person would do this. Speaking in tongues was granted to impress the unbeliever with the wonderful works of God!

I. A Scriptural Study Of The Meaning Of This Concept Will Now Be Presented.

   A. The case of the first usage of this concept, Acts 2:1-11.

      1. I will belabor this point since the charismatic people generally would have us to believe this was a heavenly language.

      2. But the Scriptures will show us that tongues refer to the languages spoken by various groups of people.

      3. Verse four says that they all spoke with tongues (γλῶσσα) as the Spirit gave them utterance.

      4. Verse eight tells us that everyone HEARD (ʼακούμεν) in his own dialect (δίαλεκτος) wherein he was born. We notice this also in verse six.

a. The word dialect, listed in Webster's dictionary, tells us that it comes from the Greek word (δίαλεκτος), and refers to the regional variations that occur when a certain language is spoken.

b. We say, he has a Bostonian accent, or he has a Maine accent, or he has a southern accent.

c. These people were hearing the Gospel preached to them in the dialect of their own particular regional language that in all probability included even the nuances of that region also.

d. When used Biblically this was indeed a marvelous gift!

5. Verse eleven says we do hear them speak in our own tongues (γλῶσσα) the wonderful works of God.

6. Verses nine through eleven list the dialects that were used on that day. I count sixteen, all either Jews or proselytes.

a. The listing of the various dialects spoken:

"And how hear we every man in our own tongue, wherein we were born? Parthians, and Medes, and Elamities, and the dwellers in Mesopotamia, and in Judaea, and Cappadocia, in Pontus, and Asia, Phrygia, and Pamphylia, in Egypt, and in the parts of Libya about Cyrene, and strangers of Rome, Jews and proselytes, Cretes and Arabians, we do hear them speak in our tongues the wonderful works of God," Acts 2:8-11.

b. Add the fact that verse seven tells us that those who spoke were Galilaeans.

c. One other point needs to be stressed: every man heard in his own tongue wherein he was born, Acts 2:8.

7. The first usage of tongues dealt with speaking in KNOWN DIALECTS!

B. The case of the general usage of the word tongue.

Each passage that follows will translate the word (γλῶσσα) tongue or tongues.

1. Revelation 5:9b, *"and hast redeemed us to God by thy blood out of every kindred, and tongue, and people, and nation."*
2. Revelation 7:9, *"After this I beheld, and, lo, a great multitude, which no man could number, of all nations, and kindreds, and people, and tongues."*
3. Revelation 13:7b, *"And power was given him over all kindreds, and tongues, nations."*
4. Revelation 14:6c, *"and to every nation, and kindred, and tongue, and people."*
5. Revelation 17:15b, *"Are people, and multitudes, and nations, and tongues."*
6. The unanimous witness of these passages teaches us that the word (γλῶσσα) refers to languages of the earth.

C. The usage of the word in the Greek language.

1. Hesiodes in his *OPERA IN DIES* 709, III B. C. uses this word to refer to the love of talking.
2. Theognis, *TRAGICUS* 63, VI B. C. used it to refer to frankness of speech.
3. Herodotus, *HISTORICUS* 1:57, V B. C. uses it to refer to a language or dialect.
4. And the translators of the Septuaginta, the Greek Old Testament, used it to translate the Genesis 11:7 word, language, by the Greek word, γλῶσσα. Of course you understand that the Septuaginta was the Greek translation of the Hebrew Old Testament which took place about 280-180 B. C. I'm sure that the Greek translators knew what the Hebrew word, הפש, meant, and translated it perfectly. Would you argue with the seventy Greek scholars who did this work? I certainly would not! In fact, if you would carefully

read verses one through eight of chapter eleven in Genesis you wouldn't have any doubt at all about what I have just been trying to show you.

D. The case at Corinth.
1. In I Corinthians 13:1 we read about the possibility of speaking with the tongues of angels.
    a. First of all we need to note that this is a statement of contrast: If I could do this, it still would be nothing of value if I had not love.
    b. If I could do this it would not be the gift of tongues referred to in I Corinthians 12:10.
    c. The gift of tongues was a sign to the unbeliever—the angels, in this case, are all believers! YES, ALL BELIEVERS!
    d. Therefore the Holy Spirit would never allow me to misuse His gift in this manner.
2. Verse two of chapter fourteen seems to imply a heavenly language also.
    a. The speaker speaks a language not known to those who are hearing him speak.
    b. God is the only one who understands what he says.
    c. He may even be revealing mysteries as he speaks.
    d. A mystery is a spiritual truth not fully known in the Old Testament time period.
    e. Let me illustrate this for you: "ὀύτωσ γάρ 'ηγάπησεν ὁ Θεὸσ τὸν κόσμον ὥστε τὸν υἱὸν 'ατοῦ τὸν μονογενῆ 'έδωκεν ἵνα πᾶσ ὁ πιστεύων είσ αὐτὸν μὴ 'απόληται 'αλλ' 'έχν ζωήν αἰώνον."
    f. Now I revealed a mystery to you, and I understood what I said—so did God, but most of you did not.

g. This is what this verse is talking about!
   1.) It is written in the Greek language.
   2.) It is John 3:16 that was being quoted.
   3.) And it is a mystery revealed in the New Testament, but not fully understood in the Old Testament.
3. Verse four of chapter fourteen could not refer to a language the speaker did not understand for our verse says, that he was edified by his speaking to himself.
   a. Edification comes only from understanding the Word of God!
   b. There is NO edification if there is No understanding!
4. Verses seven through twelve of chapter fourteen give us some very good information about this subject.
   a. We learn from verse seven that a distinction must always be discernable, otherwise we will not know what to do, neither will anyone else.
   b. Verse eight cites an example for us: the trumpet must always give a certain sound. In the days of yesteryear the trumpet would sound reveille and everyone would know that it was time to get up, the trumpeter would play taps and everyone would know to go to bed, and he would sound charge or retreat so that the combatants would know what to do. There could be no uncertainty at all.
   c. Verse nine makes an application for us: unless we speak so that our hearers understand what we are saying they will not know what to do.
   d. Verse ten gives us a summary statement: every voice whether of man, or beast, or fowl, or creeping thing, or thing blown, or strummed, or struck must communicate so that the hearer understands what is being said, cheeped, barked, meowed, or sung, or played, or stroked.

  e. Verse eleven draws a conclusion for us: If the above is not true, then all hope of communication is lost.

  f. And verse twelve sets forth a principle: If you want to be a success in doing the Lord's work, then seek to excel in what will edify the church!

  5. Verse thirteen of chapter fourteen tells us that tongues need to be interpreted, and that prayer should be made so that this can be done.

  a. If they can be interpreted, they must be known languages.

  b. Remember, tongues are a sign to the unbeliever.

  6. Verse fourteen of chapter fourteen says that if I pray in a tongue I do not understand that it will profit me nothing!

  a. If I could pray in a tongue that I did not understand, even if it were a heavenly language, it would result in unfruitfulness in my life.

  b. If it were unknown to me I would be a fool to pray in it lest I pray an unscriptural prayer.

  c. How does the Apostle Paul solve this problem? He says, "*I will pray with spirit, and I will pray with the understanding also: I will sing with the spirit, and I will sing with the understanding also,*" I Corinthians 14:15.

  d. Can you improve upon his solution? Then by all means use it!

E. Some summary statements:

  1. Scripture is the best interpreter of Scripture.

  2. The first usage, the general usage, the common Greek usage, and even every passage in chapter fourteen requires us to translate (γλῶσσ) as a known and spoken language.

  3. It is just as great a sin to add to the Word as it is to take away from the Word!

II. A Scriptural Explanation Of The Words, UNKNOWN and OTHER.
   A. Unknown, I Corinthians 14:2, 4, 13, 14, 19, 27.
      1. This word was added by the translators to show that the language being spoken was not known by the speaker prior to him having received the gift to speak it.
      2. It was a known language to the hearers since they heard in their own dialect the wonderful Words of God.
      3. Only in the secondary sense was it used to refer to a language that the hearers did not understand—it was unknown to the speaker before the Holy Spirit enabled him to speak the language of the hearers.
      4. Notice the italics in your Bible. This indicates that the word unknown was not in the original manuscripts.
      5. Literally speaking the word unknown must be left out every time we find it used with the word tongue.
   B. Other, I Corinthians 14:21.
      1. This refers to a language other than ones native tongue.
      2. God said that He would speak to His people, who spoke Hebrew, through people who spoke other known languages as their native tongues. This is what our missionaries are doing today.
      3. But all people understand the Gospel when it is presented to them in their native tongue, Acts 22:2. This is the reason I like to use a person from the country I am ministering in as my translator rather than using even the missionary who is working in that field. But I have used a number of missionaries who were excellent translators.
      4. This is the second lesson in this series of four lessons on this subject. We have already given you more than enough material to convince every open-minded person that tongue speaking is not for them. But if you still have a problem I would challenge you to pray about it, and be sure to study with me the next two lessons on the subject.

Scripture Text: I Corinthians 12:10.

Theme: A More Excellent Way.

Title: Divers Kinds Of Tongues, VIII-c.

Introduction: In our previous lesson in this series of four lessons on speaking in tongues we studied how the word tongues was used in the Bible, and gave a brief explanation of how the words unknown and other were used. Now in this lesson we will ask seven times if speaking in tongues would be profitable for you and me, and we shall answer with seven emphatic Scriptural NOs! Then we shall conclude with some summary statements that I trust will profit us all.

I. IS SPEAKING IN TONGUES PROFITABLE FOR ME?

   A. No, Because There Is A More Excellent Way!

      1. The Corinthians sought the showy gifts so that all who saw them would think they were spiritual people.

      2. But the Apostle Paul recommends that they seek the gifts that would edify the whole church, I Corinthians 14:12.

      3. It takes No effort, No labor, and No prayer time to speak in tongues, but to do the work of the Lord it takes all of the above and more.

      4. The more excellent way brings glory to God while the less excellent way brings glory to man if used wrongly.

      5. The more excellent way seeks God's will first, it does God's work God's way, and it glorifies Him as it edifies His Church.

   B. No, Because It Is The Least Of All The Gifts, I Corinthians 12:28.

      1. Even helps and governments are of more value to me as a worker for Christ than being able to speak in tongues.

      2. Helps and governments are never mentioned by those involved in the charismatic movement as signs of being filled with the Holy Spirit. I wonder why? Do you wonder why?

3. Could it be they demand that those who have them be involved in true Christian toil where there is little or no praise, recognition, or glory?
4. All other gifts are more profitable to me than speaking in tongues. Why then would anyone seek to speak in tongues to the exclusion of all the other gifts?
5. Are they led by the flesh instead of the Spirit they claim to be filled with?

C. No, Because This Gift Will Cease, I Corinthians 13:8.
1. Tongues will cease as a sign to the unbeliever is what the above Scripture tells us.
2. They will cease or stop in and of themselves because their purpose will have been fulfilled.
3. Since they shall cease they are of less value to me than those gifts that shall not cease.
4. They ceased at the close of the first century when the Bible was completed, and when the sign seeking nation Israel was set aside is my honest belief.
5. What if I sought to speak in tongues all my life, and finally was able to do it right now, and they ceased five minutes later? What profit would I have received?
6. They have failed I believe, otherwise every Christian missionary going to the mission field would not have to study a foreign language.
7. What a deceitful thing it is to say that a gift is available when it is not, and everyone knows that it is not, even those who falsely claim that it is. How utterly disappointed I would be as a missionary if I had been taught that this gift was available, but I still had to spend years in language school before I could go to the foreign mission field!

D. No, Because Other Gifts Are Of An Abiding Nature.
1. Love will never fail, nor cease—it abides forever!

2. Faith, hope, and love are profitable to me since they abide forever.
3. Biblical faith whether it is gift faith, or Word faith causes me to walk with God, hope causes me to expect to receive all that the Word promises me, and love empowers me to love others even as He loved me.
4. Now honestly, before God, wouldn't you rather have an abiding gift rather than a temporary one regardless of how showy it may be?

E. No, Because Even Praying In Tongues Is Unprofitable, 14:15.
1. First of all you cannot profit from my praying in an unknown tongue, thus I am not edifying you or the church.
2. Secondly, if I could pray in a tongue that I didn't understand myself, then I would not profit from my own praying. How ridiculous this would be!
3. My whole life would be characterized by unfruitfulness since I would never know how to put legs to the prayers that I had prayed without understanding.
4. The pray of faith shall be heard. Where is my faith if I know not what I asked for? How could I ever rejoice in an answered prayer if I never knew what I had prayed for?
5. Don't be beguiled by the trickery with which the fleshly deceiver has been duped by his own deceptive practices.
6. Believe in God, His Word, His Son, and His Holy Spirit for you will never need more than these.

F. No, Because It Does Little For The Church.
1. The gift of tongues was a sign for the unbeliever, I Corinthians 14:22
   a. It was a sign to help their unbelief.
   b. The church is made up of believers only!
   c. How then could this gift help the church?

d. It could not, and should never be practiced in the church, 14:23.

e. Look at the damage this practice has done to the churches you know of in your own area alone.

2. A tongue speaker edified himself, not the church, 14:4.

   a. For he promotes himself among the brethren by showing off his gift like I will now do by giving your two passages from the Bible, one in Greek and the other one in Hebrew. "'εν 'αρχῇ 'ην ὁ λόγος καὶ ὁ λόγος 'η πρὰς τὸν θεόν" "תישארב ארב לא םיה תא םימשה תאו ץראה"

   b. Aren't you impressed with my ability to write in two foreign languages? I learned each one, I did not receive either one as a gift from the Holy Spirit.

   c. Your understanding was fruitless even though I was writing great Biblical truths unto you. I was writing from John 1:1 and Genesis 1:1.

   d. Only a self-centered, fleshly individual would continue to do this in the church, even if he does have a so-called interpreter with him.

   e. And if he could write in English, then why would he write in any other language?

3. Prophesying is much better than speaking in tongues, I Corinthians 14:1-4, 19.

   a. Prophesying here refers to the setting forth of the prophecies that have been given already, and regular preaching.

   b. This edifies the whole church, it exhorts the whole church, and it comforts the whole church.

   c. Only a very selfish person would seek, to edify himself at the expense of the whole church, but that is what a tongue speaker does when he speaks in tongues in the church.

4. Speaking only five words with your understanding in a language that your hearers understand would be far better than speaking ten thousand words in a language that they did not understand, I Corinthians 14:19.

   a. Did you hear what Paul just said to the church at Corinth?

   b. It was so clear that even I understood what he said. Did you understand what the Scripture said?

   c. It was so clear that any person who will accept what the Bible teaches could understand it.

   d. Why, even a first grade student in our school could understand it!

   e. A simple devotion by the youngest person in the Lord would be of more value to the church than the greatest message ever preached in a foreign language if the church could not understand it.

   f. Preaching edifies, exhorts, and comforts the church, but tongue speaking does not!

5. Tongue speaking promotes uncertainty, 14:7-12.

   a. For a clear distinction is not always made, 14:7.

   b. For a good example is not always given, 14:8.

   c. For a proper application is not always made, 14:9

   d. For a complete summary is not always given, 14:10.

   e. For an adequate conclusion is not always reached, 14:11.

   f. For a Biblical principle is not always set forth, 14:12.

   g. For a Scriptural illustration is not always given:

      1.) If I say unto you, βαίνω, do you understand?

      2.) If I say in another language, אוּב, do you now understand?

      3.) You see, my writing in other languages has brought confusion into our midst when I could have written it in English, and we all could have understood.

6. Tongue speaking promotes disorder, 14:23.
   a. I well remember those days as a young man seeing those "spirit filled" individuals interrupt the preacher as he was presenting the Word of God.
   b. God was not the author of that confusion!
   c. Nothing should ever take precedence over the preaching of the Word of God! ABSOLUTELY NOTHING!
G. Tongue Speaking Was Not The Choice Of The Apostle Paul For Me Either, I Corinthians 14:1-3, *"Follow after charity, and desire spiritual gifts, but rather that ye may prophesy. For he that speaketh in an unknown tongue speaketh not unto men, but unto God: for no man underestandeth him; howbeit in the spirit he speaketh mysteries. But he that prophesieth speaketh unto men to edification, and exhortation, and comfort."*
   1. Just mull over these verses for a few minutes then understand that God understands whatever language we are speaking. Let me say it again, He understands whatever language we are speaking!
   2. Then pray that you will understand what Paul has said to you as he speaks to the believers at Corinth.

II. ARE TONGUES FOR EVERYONE?
   A. No, Because They Are Given By The Holy Spirit As He Wills, I Corinthians 12:11.
   B. No, Because The Scriptures Tell Us That They Are Not, I Corinthians 12:29, 30.
   C. No, Because Men Have Been Spirit Filled And Have Not Spoken In Tongues, Acts 4:8, 13:9.
      1. How then can this be a sign that you are Spirit filled?
      2. It was a sign in some cases, but not in all cases.

3. Christ was Spirit filled, and so was John the Baptist, but neither of them spoke in tongues.
4. Tongue speaking was a new thing that lasted until the Word was completed, after that it ceased.
5. All that tongue speaking ever signified was that you had the gift of tongues.
6. And all that so-called tongue speaking ever signified was that the speaker was out of fellowship with the Lord, if he ever knew the Lord.
7. The Holy Spirit would never lead me to speak in tongues among believers for this would contradict the expressed purpose of tongues. The Spirit never contradicts the Word that He has revealed unto us. The Spirit filled person never contradicts the Word either. Those who do are not Spirit filled, but controlled by the flesh. Speak words easily understood to those who hear you, and you'll have God's blessings on you and your ministry!

Scripture Text: I Corinthians 12:10.

Theme: A More Excellent Way.

Title: Drivers Kinds Of Tongues, VIII-d.

Introduction: With this lesson we conclude our series on "Speaking In Tongues." We have not been exhaustive in our study, but at least, we have exposed you to the subject. I trust that as we consider the rules for speaking in tongues, the characteristics of those who speak in tongues, the true fruit of the Spirit, and whether we can forbid anyone to speak in tongues that we shall all be better informed concerning this movement.

I. WHAT ARE THE RULES FOR SPEAKING IN TONGUES?

   A. Let All Things Be Done Unto Edifying, I Corinthians 14:26c.

      1. The church at Corinth had men who thought they were spiritual, but they were not---they were carnal!

      2. Evidently they took over the control of the church services, and put self on display instead of Almighty God.

      3. Thus no one received anything that strengthened his faith in the things of the Lord when this happened.

         a. If the unlearned ('ιδιῶται-uninstructed) were present they could not learn 23a.

         b. If the unbelieving were present they would think the whole congregation was mad, 23b.

         c. Tongues were to reach the unbelievers outside the local church situation, 22a.

      4. Tongues were not to be used in the ordinary church service where all spoke one tongue, 22b and 24.

         a. This was true even when unbelievers were present, and especially if the unbelievers spoke your language.

         b. It is the preaching of the Gospel that saves the poor lost sinner.

         c. It is the preaching of the Gospel that edifies the saints of God.

B. Let All Things Be Done Decently And In Order, 40.
 1. Speaking in tongues must be orderly, 27.
    a. Only three on any occasion could speak in this way in the Church.
    b. It must be by course, one after another.
    c. One must interpret, or else the speaker was to remain silent, 28.
 2. Speaking in tongues must not promote confusion, 33.
    a. Peace should be the characteristic of a godly church service.
    b. Confusion means a state of great disorder, or a deranged mental condition exists that is promoted by Satan.
    c. In some holiness meeting the latter is sometimes the rule rather than the exception, I said some, not all.
 3. Speaking in tongues for women is forbidden, 34.
    a. Here the word is (λαλεῖν), and it means to speak.
    b. Also (σιγάωσαν) means to be silent.
    c. How then can women speak at all in the church?
    d. They cannot teach the congregation, nor can they speak with other tongues.
    e. How many women speak, teach, and preach within the charismatic movement? A few? A lot? Multitudes?
 4. Speaking in tongues does not make you spiritual, but OBEDIENCE DOES!
    a. Truly Spirit filled people obey the rules of God because they understand why God gave the rules in the first place!
    b. How many tongues speakers abide by the rules?

II. WHAT ARE THE CHARACTERISTICS OF TONGUE SPEAKERS?
   A. They Usually Develop A Spiritual Superiority Complex.
      1. I was told by one individual that he and his kind were so far ahead of the rest of us, spiritually, that you could not even imagine how far ahead of us they were.
      2. The same man failed to correct the sin that was in his life for a long time.
      3. If you do not speak in tongues, you are not Spirit filled has been the statement of many of this persuasion.
      4. Spirit filled people are honest people all the time.
      5. Dishonest people cannot, and never can be Spirit filled people until they empty themselves of self by confession that sin to God and asking Him to forgive them of it.
   B. They Often Keep Their Favorite Worldly Habits.
      1. Some use bad language, some cheat at work, some do not pay their bills, and some are very critical.
      2. They do what is right in their own eyes that have been clouded over by their blindness to their own sin.
      3. Is this a Spirit filled believer's walk?
   C. They Also Become Unteachable.
      1. Who are you to tell me anything, you don't even have the gift, is the answer I get more often than not.
      2. Fall on your knees and ask God for it brother, and then come and talk to me is another answer.
      3. Then when I show them what I Corinthians 12:11 says they reply, yes, but we have the hidden meaning of that passage. God deals with the obvious meaning of any passage when the obvious meaning is obvious to me is my reply.
      4. And then there is this statement, God has given me a new revelation even though it contradicts the Bible. That will never happen, ever!

- D. They Have A Tendency To Split Churches.
    1. Churches must develop unity around the Word of God, and this means accepting it as it is given by God.
    2. Tongues develop unity around an individual.
    3. And then the individual splits the church, next the splits splinter, and splinters split again, and the congregation gets thinner and thinner so that in the end the devil is winner.
- E. They Belittle Teaching And Preaching With Their Tongue Speaking.
    1. Teaching is greater by far than tongue speaking, I Corinthians 12:28, and so is preaching, 14:19.
    2. But those who speak in tongues often interrupt the teaching or preaching ministry that goes on in the church.
    3. How foolish is the person who stops the teaching or preaching messages about Christ to relate some experience that he has had, especially relating it in an unknown tongue that is babble rather than Scripture.
- F. They Often Burn Out As Quickly As They Were Ignited.
    1. A balloon is puffed up with hot air, big on the outside with nothing on the inside. Were the Corinthians puffed up or not?
    2. One little hole deflates the whole bag of air.
    3. When those who abuse the gifts that God has given to the church can't get up anymore they are done for, forever.
    4. Have you ever tried to revive a burned out Christian?
    5. Well, those who have been super inflated are almost impossible to revive again.
- G. They Bring Into One Camp People Of All Faiths.
    1. That's great isn't? No, it should be all people of the one faith.
    2. Christ deniers, blasphemers, immoral persons, and Bible deniers cannot have sweet fellowship in Jesus even though they all may claim to be believers.

3. A Spirit filled person believes it all, and tries to obey it all, and that with all of his heart.

4. We need to unify, that is for sure, but it must be unity based on the Word of God—not on the flesh.

III. HOW DOES THE TONGUE SPEAKER COMPARE WITH THE SPIRIT FILLED PERSON?

A. Notice The Fruit Of The Spirit, Galatians 5:22-23, *"But the fruit of the Spirit is love, joy, peace, longsuffering, gentleness, goodness, faith, meekness, temperance: against such there is no law."*

1. You see there is no tongue speaking listed here as one of the fruits a Spirit filled person bears.

2. Tongue speaking is a gift of the Holy Spirit that He gives only to those He wills to receive it.

3. Surely if tongue speaking came because a person was filled with the Holy Spirit it would be listed in this passage.

B. Notice the devotion of those who are Christ's, *"And they that are Christ's have crucified the flesh with the affections and lusts,"* Galatians 5:24.

1. They have put to death the flesh with the affections and lusts so that they desire only that which God desires them to have.

2. They desire the useful gifts, not the showy ones.

3. They exalt Christ, not self for self has been put to death.

C. Notice The Walk Of Those Who Are Spirit Filled, Galatians 5:25, *"If we live in the Spirit, let us also walk in the Spirit."*

1. When I walk in the Spirit He controls me.

2. His job is to glorify Christ, John 15:26, 16:13, 14, and so is mine.

3. In Word and deed it is Christ for me, Colossians 3:17.

D. Notice The Desire Of The Spirit Filled Person, Galatians 5:26, *"Let us not be desirous of vain glory, provoking one another, envying one another."*

1. He is not desirous of vainglory because all is done for Christ's glory—all done for self would be vainglory.
2. To provoke here would be using our vainglory to upset another person by our bragging about our spirituality.
3. And not envying one who has a higher position would demonstrate our willingness to be content with the things that God has given to us.

IV. MAY I FORBID ONE TO SPEAK IN TONGUES?

A. No, If They Still Continue Unto This Day, I Corinthians 14:39b.
   1. This statement is clear and is easy to understand.
   2. I may command however that the rules for speaking in tongues be observed.
   3. When the rules are applied as they are given in the Bible the gift of speaking in tongues seems to strangely disappear.
   4. Would it be vainglory to seek the gift when the Bible tells us that the Holy Spirit gives it to whomsoever He wills?

B. Yes, If The Gift Has Ceased.
   1. The Jews who sought the sign are gone as separated from the plan of God as a nation, Colossians 3:11, I Corinthians 14:21.
   2. Scripture says tongues will cease, I Corinthians 13:8.
   3. History shows they ceased not long after the lasts days began as noted in Acts 2:16-20.
   4. The revelation of God is now complete-- we have it all! God has givens all that we will EVER need!

Brothers and sisters be mature in the Lord Jesus Christ, witness and testify for Him and you'll never become so spiritually dead that you'll grasp at a false hope that is built on a false teaching that is promoted by a false prophet. This will not happen if you are continually being filled with the Holy Spirit, Ephesians 5:18.

Scripture Text: I Corinthians 12:10.

Theme: A More Excellent Way.

Title: The Interpretation Of Tongues, IX.

Introduction: This lesson brings to a close our study of the so-called nine charismatic gifts listed in I Corinthians 12:8-10. It will be briefer in content and length because of its very nature that should be easy to understand. However, there are some very important facts that we need to be aware of relating to the exercise of this gift. Let us therefore get to the task before us as we notice:

I. THIS IS THAT SPECIAL ABILITY TO INTERPRET A FOREIGN LANGUAGE THAT WE DID NOT KNOW PRIOR TO THE OCCASION ON WHICH IT WAS USED (ἑρμηνεία γλωσσῶν).

II. IT WOULD BE USED WHEN A FOREIGNER WOULD COME TO SPEAK TO US, BUT HE DID NOT KNOW OUR LANGUAGE, THEN GOD WOULD GIVE ONE OF US THE ABILITY TO INTERPRET WHAT HE WAS SAYING IN HIS LANGUAGE INTO OUR LANGUAGE SO WE COULD UNDERSTAND WHAT HE HAD SAID.

III. GOD GAVE CERTAIN ONES THE SPECIAL ABILITY TO TRANSLATE WITHOUT HAVING TO FIRST LEARN THAT LANGUAGE.

IV. THE WHOLE CONCEPT OF SPEAKING IN TONGUES IN YOUR OWN CHURCH, AND THEN HAVING ANOTHER MEMBER OR GUEST INTREPRET WHAT YOU HAD SAID IS COMPLETELY FOREIGN TO SCRIPTURE.

   A. This Is A Devilish Practice Conceived By Evil Men Who Seek To Deceive Their People, And Elevate Themselves.

   B. They Were To Always Speak The Language Of Their Own People So That Their People Could Profit From It.

C. Even Five Words Which Could Be Understood Would Be Better Than Ten Thousand Words In A Foreign Language Which Could Not Be Understood, Or Had To Be Interpreted Because It Was A Set-Up Situation, I Corinthians 14:19.

V. BEFORE I CLOSE THIS DISCUSSION I NEED TO CLARIFY SOME CONCEPTS FOR YOU.

A. Six Important Closing Statements.

1. I can interpret what others have said from their own language to your language if I can speak both languages. Raul Kling did this for me when I was in Romania. He spoke English and Romanian. Thus he interpreted what I was saying in English into the Romanian language so the Romanians could understand what I had said.

2. I can interpret the meaning of the words I am speaking so that you not only hear the words, but also know the meaning of the words I am speaking. When I was in Portugal speaking to a multi-language group (French, Angolan Portuguese, Brazilian Portuguese, and Portugian Portuguese, English, and Armenian) I used the word *gentle* in a statement, but no one there understood its meaning, and my translator did not know how to translate its meaning. Thus I had to illustrate its meaning by picturing a giant of a man holding a newborn baby in his enormous arms, and saying he was *gentle* with the child, then they all understood!

3. I can also translate one language into as many other languages as I know. The meaning is basically the same when we say translate or interpret!

4. However, when we draw the bottom line translating or interpreting always refers to one person having the learned ability or the supernatural ability to take one known language and give its meaning into another known language.

5. I've had an interpreter with me in Israel, Lebanon, French Canada, Cypress, Egypt, Greece, Italy, Turkey, Holland, Portugal, Hungary, Germany, Austria, Romania, and Mexico, but I've never been able to speak a language I had not learned.

6. Thank God for those who labor so they can speak in more than one known language in order that we who struggle with our own native tongue may converse with those who know not our own local dialect.

THE PAUSE THAT ENLIGHTENS:

Now and then we need to stop and refresh our memories as to what we have learned already.

I. First we learned that we do not have a definite statement in the Bible that the charismatic gifts we have been studying have passed away.

II. However, we did learn that one will be done away with, one will cease, and that one will vanish away, I Corinthians 13:8.

III. But even here we are not told when these three things will happen.

IV. Nevertheless we are told that the Holy Spirit is the giver of all these gifts, that He gives them only as He wills, when He wills, and to whomsoever He wills.

V. I think that we also learned that the gifts were to be used to edify the believer, or to be a sign unto the unbeliever, I Corinthians 14:4, 22.

VI. We have also looked for an adequate provision when and should these gifts cease—it is my personal belief that they have all ceased for one and only one reason: there was no more need for them once the Bible was completed for it became their all-sufficient rule for their faith and practice!

VII. Now let us consider the contrast between the two:

Gift Source, the Holy Spirit I Corinthians 12:11	Provision Source, the Bible plus the illuminatory work of the Holy Spirit.
1. There is a dividing---- διαροῦν	1. There is no dividing.
2. It is done separately---ἰδία	2. Nothing done separately.
3. It is to each-------------ἑκάστῳ	3. It is to all who seek.
4. It is according to the --καθὼς-- Holy Spirit's will.	4. It is according to God's working through man.
5. As he wills--------------βούλεται	5. It is up to man to use what God has provided.

VIII. Now I want to do one more thing with you for your own satisfaction. We'll begin to look at the gifts listed in I Corinthians 12:4-10, and ask some questions about each allowing you to make your own decision as to whether you will seek the gift or use the provision. We'll begin with the last one and work our way back to the first one.

9. Interpretation of tongues?

   a. Do we have this gift today?

   b. Did it cease when tongues ceased?

   c. Does Scripture tell us it will cease, fail, or vanish?

   d. Why then are we not using it?

   e. Is it used today Scripturally?

   f. Do we need it today?

   g. Why then are not translators using it?

   h. Do we have a Scriptural provision to replace it?

8. Divers kinds of tongues.

   a. Does the Bible teach us that they will cease?

   b. Have they ceased?

   c. Why do we believe that they have ceased?

d. Is it because the Bible is now complete?
   e. Any other reason?
   f. Is there a provision for their replacement?
7. Discerning of spirits.
   a. Do we have this gift today?
   b. What can this gift give us vs. our provision?
   c. What can our provision give us over the gift?
   d. Why then would you seek this gift?
   e. Could it be because the provision is not being used?
6. Prophecy.
   a. Do we believe that we have this gift today?
   b. What new prophecy has been added to your Bible?
   c. Of all those who claim to be prophets giving prophecies which one do you accept?
   d. Could it be that we now have all the prophecies we need?
   e. If so, who needs this gift of prophecy?
   f. Does the Bible say that prophecies will cease?
   g. What provision has God made to replace prophecy?
5. Miracles.
   a. Do we still have this gift today?
   b. Have the message and the messengers been authenticated?
   c. What sign or wonder do you need to believe the Bible?
   d. What bearing does John 20:30, 31 have on your answer?
   e. Does God still do supernatural things?

f. Is there any Biblical provision given to replace miracles?
4. Healings.
   a. Do we have this gift today?
   b. Is this gift used Biblically today?
   c. Can you point out the errors of false usage?
   d. Why do people believe in it?
   e. Is there a provision to replace this gift?
3. Faith.
   a. Does Scripture talk about how to obtain faith?
   b. Is there any inadequacy in this provision?
   c. What could the gift do for you that the provision could not give you?
   d. What can the provision do for you that the gift couldn't?
   e. Which one will you pursue?
2. Knowledge.
   a. Where do I learn that this gift will vanish?
   b. When did it vanish?
   c. Do we have an adequate source of knowledge in the Bible?
   d. Which will you pursue, the gift or the provision?
   e. Why?
1. Wisdom.
   a. What is God's provision to replace this gift?
   b. Is there any limit to my asking?
   c. How does God give to me when I ask?
   d. Will He make fun of me for asking?

e. Tell me what the gift could do for you that the provision could not do.

In conclusion: Please check and see how many of these gifts you have available to you that are as good as the provision that God has made for you in His Holy Word. We have noticed that three will pass away in one form or another (tongues, prophecy, knowledge), that we question legitimately the practice of three more (miracles, healings, and interpretation of tongues), and that the last three have adequate provisions made in the Word for their replacement (wisdom, faith, and discerning of spirits). Tell me then, why these gifts are still being pursued as they are today?

Your answer please!

Wow! Did you learn as much as I did studying these nine gifts? Do you begin to see now why our brother Paul tells us to covet the More Excellent way? If not, then I trust that the next three sections will provide sufficient information to convince you that the More Excellent Way is God's will for our lives.

SECTION FOUR

Scripture Text: Romans 12:6-8

SECTION FOUR: Scripture Text: Romans 12:6-8.

Theme: A More Excellent Way.

Title: The Gifts, Their Proper Use.

Introduction: Turn with me now to Romans 12:6-8 where we learn from Scripture how we are to use the gift God has given to us in particular. We are not to compare ourselves with others, especially as it relates to gifts. All spiritual gifts are given to us by God, that when used properly, we put forth a united effort against our common enemy, the devil.

Now in doing this we must remember that God gives gifts, abilities, talents, and charisma to us according to our ability to use them (Matthew 25:15), and that He then judges us as to how we used what He has given to us (Matthew 25:19-30). Thus our concern then should not be on what others have, but we do not. It should be focused on how well we are using what we have received from God.

Can you even begin to visualize how awesome the Church of Jesus Christ would be if everyone who has received a gift would use it to compliment all those others who have gifts? There would be no competitiveness between God's children as they seek to serve the One who gave them their gifts! There would be no lack to any child of God as he/she sought to do the work of God for all the other gifted brothers and sisters in Christ would supply every need that surfaced! There would be no victories for the devil for he could not overcome such a united force! And the holy Church Of Jesus Christ would be presented, in all its resplendent glory, to a world that desperately needs to see the Church as God intended it to be seen from its inception! I think this is the reason that the Apostle Paul inserted I Corinthians 12:12-27 between 12:1-11 and 12:28-31. The Body of Christ should work together like all the parts of the human body work together for the common good of the whole! Will it ever be so? It could start with you and me!

In the verses before us the above truths, I trust, will be crystal clear so that we do our very best with what God has given us to serve Him. We will never come up short on the Judgment Day if we do this.

I. WE HAVE DIFFERING GIFTS, BUT ALL COME FROM THE SAME GOD.
   A. The Differing Gifts (χαρίσματα διάφορα) Summarized.
      1. We will have looked at about twenty-four different gifts when this study is over.
      2. But each one seems to have a distinctive function even though it may have some similar traits with some other gifts: pastors can teach and do evangelistic work.
      3. They differ because they were designed by God to meet different needs under varying circumstance.
      4. Thus our responsibility is to discern what God has given us to use then use it for His glory.
   B. The Differing Gifts Have A Common Source.
      1. They come to us by the grace of God.
      2. The grace of God has often been defined as: God's Riches At Christ's Expense.
      3. It took Jesus' death on Calvary's cross in order for you and me to receive any of the gifts of God.
      4. Notice the similarity between the following verses:
         a. Ephesians 2:8, *"For by grace are ye saved."*
         b. Romans 12:6, *"according to the grace that is given us."*
      5. Do you now see why God alone can give gifts to us?
      6. And do you now understand why each gift must be used with the greatest care?

II. THE DIFFERING GIFTS LISTED AND EXPLAINED IN THIS PASSAGE.

   A. Prophecy (προφητείαν) is to be done according to the proportion of faith that we have.

      1. Since some prophets will have a greater prophetic ministry than other prophets (major prophets vs. minor prophets) it is necessary that each one who has the gift of prophecy use it to its fullest extent, but not beyond its fullest extent.

      2. One prophet must not compete with another prophet, but he must compliment the other's ministry.

      3. This relates to the foretelling and the forth-telling ministry of every prophet.

   B. Ministering (διακονίαν), let us wait on our ministering.

      1. The word translated, ministry, refers to service rendered to those in need.

      2. Therefore we are to wait on our ministering so that it becomes our main avenue of service.

      3. For those having the gift of serving, serving should be considered their best way to please God.

   C. He That Teacheth (διδάσκων) is to focus on teaching.

      1. Let me quickly remind you that according to God's hierarchy of gifts teaching is number one now that the apostles and prophets are no longer with us, I Corinthians 12:28.

      2. Teaching is to be the number one priority for those who have this gift of teaching.

   D. He That Exhorteth (παρακλήσει), on exhortation.

      1. There is no one who can minister to those who need to be lifted up better than the one who has the gift of exhortation.

      2. He/she is better equipped to encourage others than even those with other gifts.

3. Once this is accepted the one who has the gift of exhortation will be completely satisfied with it even if it is the only gift he/she receives.

E. He That Giveth (μεταδιδούς) let him do it with simplicity ('απλότητι).
   1. When I give with simplicity I give from the heart.
   2. Thus I never give with any ulterior motivation.
      a. I do not do it to be known.
      b. I do not do it in hope of receiving a reward, or favor from God.
      c. I do not do it to benefit me, but to benefit the one receiving it from me.
   3. I give as God has given to me for I would have nothing to give if God had not given to me first!

F. He That Ruleth (προϊστάμενος), with diligence (σπουδῇ).
   1. Some men and women are gifted to rule, but most are not, please make a note of this.
   2. But those who are gifted to rule must rule well whether they want to or not.
   3. They must be consistent in their rule across the board whether ruling for or against friend or foe.
   4. It takes the gift of God to do this properly, but God will bless the person who is diligent in his rule.

G. He That Showeth Mercy ('ελεῶν), with cheerfulness.
   1. Mercy is holding back from someone what he/she deserves.
   2. God's mercy keeps us from being consumed, Lamentations, 3:22.
   3. It will take the gift of mercy to keep us from rendering unto others what they render unto us.
   4. But praise God I can do it, and I will do it if God gives me the gift of mercy.

Conclusion: No person receiving a gift from God can use it anyway he/she wishes to use it. He/she can use it only as God has ordained its usage. Woe, be unto the person who takes an unblemished gift from God, and uses it to bring shame upon God rather than Glory!

However, when we pursue the More Excellent Way we will always be in the center of God's will for our lives, and we will be in the place of blessing also.

SECTION FIVE

Scripture Text:
1 Peter 4:7-11

SECTION FIVE: Scripture Text: I Peter 4:7-11.

Theme: A More Excellent Way.

Title: Being The Good Stewards God Has Commanded Us To Be.

Introduction: We now turn to our next to the last passage under consideration, I Peter 4:7-11. The key verse I Peter 4:10 focuses on how in particular each gift is to be used: we are to use it as the steward of his master's household would use it. In other words, use it just like Jesus would use it in the service of His Father in heaven. Notice then:

I. THE PREREQUISITES NEEDED FOR THOSE USING A GIFT GIVEN TO ANY PERSON.

  A. Be Ye Sober (σωφρονήσατε).

   1. This requires us to be sober-minded.

   2. That is, not influenced by any outside pressures, such as: the devil, the world, or evil of any type.

   3. But be influenced by the Word of God and the Holy Spirit of God.

   4. This can be accomplished by putting Romans 12:1, 2 to work in your life on the one hand, and by following the teaching of Galatians 5:16 on the other hand.

  B. Watch Unto Prayer (νήψατε είσ τὰσ προσυχάς).

   1. The word watch exhorts us to be aware of everything that is going on around us, especially as it pertains to Biblical matters.

   2. And as we become aware of certain activities we are to go to God in prayer seeking to know the times, and how the Word applies to those times.

   3. It also warns us to be alert as to how we are to use the gifts God has given to us—use them always in all ways under the superintendence of the Holy Spirit as outlined in the Bible.

C. Have Fervent Charity.
  1. Of course, the word translated fervent needs no deep study. It means passionate or ardent action.
  2. And the word charity ('αγάπην) refers to self-sacrificing love. This is the same type of love God expressed to us when He gave Jesus for us, John 3:16.
  3. This type of love is to be expressed among brothers and sisters (είσ ἑαυτοὺσ) in Christ.
  4. The reason that fervent love is to be expressed to brothers and sisters in Christ is that it will cover (καλύψει) a multitude of sins.
     a. This does not mean that any sin will be atoned for by our fervent love for one another.
        1.) Love for the world moved God to send His Son to die in our place on the cross.
        2.) But only Christ's death on that cross could atone for our sins when they are confessed.
     b. What does this mean then? It means that we are now to look at the sins of others just like God looked at our sins.
        1.) He hated our sins!
        2.) But He loved the sinner so much that He caused Christ to die for us while we were yet sinners, Romans 5:8.
     c. In this sense fervent love causes us to see the desperate need of the heart rather than the vileness expressed through acts of sins that can be manifold, and wicked.

D. Use Hospitality One To Another Without Grudging.
  1. Now hospitality (φιλόξενοι) refers to extending brotherly affection to those who are in need, or to those who are invited into your home.
  2. This hospitality is to be extended to one another ('αλλήλουσ).
     a. Remember that the word hospitality refers to brotherly affection that is extended to others.

b. But here it refers to brotherly affection being extended by believers to those who are believers in Christ. That is what the word, 'αλλήλουσ, means—those of the same belief.
3. And it is to be done without grudging (γογγυσμῶν) or murmuring.
   a. Do not complain about the time, the expense, or the effort needed for you to extend hospitality to another believer.
   b. But do it as a good steward of the household of God for indeed it is God who has given to you that you may give to another.

II. THE CHALLENGE TO USE ANY GIFT BIBLICALLY.
   A. The Source Of The Gift Referred To In This Passage.
      1. Our passage says that it is a received gift.
      2. We are to use it as a good steward of God.
      3. It is to be used for His honor and His glory.
      4. As other Biblical gifts come from God so does this one.
   B. The Identity Of The Gift That Was Given By God.
      1. It is any one of the twenty-four, or so gifts mentioned in the passages we have or will have studied.
      2. It is that particular gift that God has given to any particular person reading this passage.
      3. It is called a gift (χαρίσμα) thus it is freely given by God to man who should use it for God's glory.
   C. The Recipients Of This Gift Given By God: as every man hath received a gift (καθὼσ 'έλαβεν χάισμα).
      1. God does not give gifts to everyone, but I believe each person is gifted in at least one area.
      2. So this message is about how in particular we are to use any gift that is given to any one of us.

D. How Are The Recipients To Use Their Gift?
1. Even so minister (διακονοῦτες) the same one to another ('εαυτοὺς).
   a. The word minister is the same word used for a deacon in the church.
   b. Thus we might say that we should minister to one another like we think a deacon should minister unto us.
2. And we are to do it also like a good steward (οἰκονόμοι) of the manifold grace of God would.
   a. In other words we should use our stewardship as if we were serving in the house of God.
   b. I Corinthians 3:16, 17 tells us that we are the temple of God.
   c. It is by the manifold grace of God that we are able to serve! What kind of service should we then render?

III. THE RULES OVER WORD AND DEED AS A GIFT IS BEING USED.
A. If Any Man Speak, as the oracles of God.
1. Of course the oracles of God refer to His Holy Word, Romans 3:1, 2.
2. Thus when a person has a gift from God he is to use that gift as it is outlined in the Bible, and he is to speak the Word of God.
B. If Any Man Minister (διακονεῖ) as of the ability ('ισχύος) which God giveth (χορηγεῖ-supplies).
1. If any man is to minister, or serve he is to assess his God given ability, then use it knowing it came from God, and that he is responsible unto God as to how he uses it.
2. Whether natural talent, or supernatural ability it all comes from God and is to be used for God, II Corinthians 4:7.

IV. THE GODLY RESULTS FLOWING OUT FROM THE BIBLICAL USE OF ANY GIFT.
   A. God, The Father Is Glorified, I Peter 4:11c.
      1. God, the Father is glorified by our proper use of any gift He has given to us.
      2. This is true because we have used His gift properly, then this proper use has helped someone else, and that someone else gives God the praise and thanks He so richly deserves.
   B. God, The Son Is Glorified, I Peter 4:11d!
      1 Now the Father is also glorified through the Son, Jesus Christ.
      2. Jesus, our Savior, is the One sent by God to save us from our sins.
      3. Only saved ones can properly use the gifts God has given.
      4. And when the saved ones use the gift, or gifts given by God properly God has the dominion and praise both now and forever!
   C. God, The Holy Spirit Is Glorified!
      1. The Holy Spirit who gave the gift or gifts is now glorified because the gifts have been used properly.
      2. What a joy we can bring to the Godhead when we do that which is ordained by them! AMEN? AMEN!

Conclusion: Are you using the gift/gifts God has given to you properly? Will you begin to use what God has given you naturally and supernaturally for His dominion, His honor, His glory, and His praise both now and forever? Then lay open your heart to Him, confess any shortcomings you have, and ask God to help you use each gift you have Scripturally.

Have you been putting it all together as we have been working through these sections? You surely have seen by now that the More Excellent Way is God's will for all of us. I say this because when you put to all together it puts us all together doing God's work, in God's way, and that for His glory.

SECTION SIX

Scripture Text:
I Corinthians 13:13

SECTION SIX: Scripture Text: I Corinthians 13:13.

Theme: A More Excellent Way.

Title: The Abiding Gifts.

Introduction: We are now ready to study our last passage under consideration. Gifts are still the theme, but we turn from the gifts and the better gifts, I Corinthians 12:31, to the More Excellent Way Paul has pointed us to some time ago. There are three gifts in this category, but they are all encompassing in scope. If you look at only how broad is the scope of love (I Corinthians 13:1-8, 13c) you will understand what I am referring to immediately. But we first must begin with FAITH!

I. THE ABIDING GIFT OF FAITH, (πίστις), 13:13a.

   A. Gift Faith Is Given By The Holy Spirit To Whomsoever He Wills And Whensoever He Wills, I Corinthians 12:9a, 11.

      1. Not everyone receives Gift Faith.

      2. Gift Faith can be given by the Holy Spirit, and taken away by Him.

      3. Gift Faith can vary from individual to individual, and from circumstance to circumstance, because He divides to every man severally.

      4. This is not an abiding gift!

   B. The Measure Of Faith Is Given By God To Each One Of Us (believers only, I believe), Romans 12:3.

      1. We are to use our measure to its fullest for the glory of God.

      2. When we do this, we will have enough faith to know and do His will for our lives.

      3. But the measure of faith is only the beginning of what we experience as it relates to full faith.

   C. Abiding Faith Is Experienced When We Act Scripturally With The Heart, The Mind, And The Soul Upon What The Word Of God Teaches, Romans 10:17.

1. We can experience as much of this kind of faith as we are willing to live out the teachings of the Word of God through our lives.
2. This is abiding faith because it is based upon the Word of God which is forever settled in heaven, and which shall never pass away, Psalm 119:89 and Matthew 5:18.
3. The word translated abides (μένει-3ps/pres/ind) means to remain, to endure, to continue, to lodge, or to continue unchanged.
4. I do not know whether you have seen why Paul calls the abiding gifts the More Excellent Way or not, but I have, and I pray that if you haven't, that you will.

II. THE ABIDING GIFT OF HOPE ('ελπίσ), 13:13b.

A. Abiding Hope Is Rooted In The Promises Of God.
1. Abiding Hope has a Biblical promise to rest upon so that we could call it our Abiding Expectation.
2. In other words, God has given us a promise upon which we can expect it to be fulfilled, thus it becomes our hope!
3. Now we could cite numerous examples of this, but we'll use only one or two so you get the picture.
    a. In John 11:25 Jesus tells Martha that even if she dies she shall live.
    b. Paul tells us that he was called unto question relating to the hope he had in the resurrection, Acts 23:6.
    c. And I Thessalonians 4:16, 17 fortifies our hope by telling us about our Rapture or Resurrection
4. Thus our hope is not based on blind faith, but on the very Word of God that abides forever.

B. Abiding Hope By Far Exceeds The Expectation Of Any Non-abiding Gift.

1. It can be renewed moment by moment by reading God's promises.
2. It can be relied upon every moment of every day because it is based on the Word of God.
3. It can be trusted because it is rooted in the promises of God that are all Yea and Amen.
4. It can be used to assure the heart when it is in doubt.
5. It can be used as a solace during troublesome times.
6. It can be shared as a testimony to others.
7. It can be used to document your faith.

III. ABIDING CHARITY ('αγάπη).
   A. Abiding Charity Or Self-Sacrificing Love Is An Expression From The Heart Of A Believer That Was Planted There By God When He Saw The Desperate Need In The Heart Of The One Needing To Receive My Self-sacrificing Love.
   B. Abiding Charity Or Self-sacrificing Love Is A Multi-faceted Type Of Gift, I Corinthians 13:1-8.
      1. It is the one gift that all other gifts must flow out from, 1-3.
      2. It has fifteen outstanding characteristics.
         a. Charity suffereth long.
         b. Charity envieth not.
         c. Charity vaunteth not itself.
         d. Charity is not puffed up.
         e. Charity doth not behave itself unseemly.
         f. Charity seeketh not her own.
         g. Charity is not easily provoked.
         h. Charity thinketh not evil.
         i. Charity rejoiceth not in iniquity.

          j. Charity rejoiceth in truth.
          k. Charity beareth all things.
          l. Charity believeth all things.
          m. Charity hopeth all things.
          n. Charity endureth all things.
          o. Charity never faileth.
      3. If you were to use this abiding gift of self-sacrificing love as laid out in the Word of God you would please God, your fellowman, and yourself.
      4. I want this abiding gift to be perfected in my life.
      5. And it can be mine anytime—for it is an abiding gift!
   C. Abiding Charity Or Self-sacrificing Love Is The Greatest Of The Abiding Gifts.
      1. Now if I am going to work on any gift, this is the one that should be of the utmost importance to me.
      2. I say this because until I have mastered this gift I'll never be able to use any other gift that will meet God's standards, I Corinthians 13:1-3.
      3. This gift will superintend my usage of all the other gifts so that God has dominion over all my gifts and their usage.
      4. When this happens all fleshly desires will vanish, all competitiveness will cease, and all glory will become God's!

In conclusion I am going to make several statements that I pray you will consider extremely important to you. However, the first statement will have a direct bearing upon all of the rest of the statements. Once you choose the path you shall walk upon it will influence you in that direction the rest of your life, and it will pursue you throughout all of eternity.

1   We shall either accept the Bible as it is, the inspired and infallible Word of God, or we shall forever be tossed to and fro

by every wind of doctrine ever learning but never coming to the knowledge of the truth.

"All scripture is given by inspiration of God, and is profitable for doctrine, for reproof, for correction, for instruction in righteousness: That the man of God may be perfect, thoroughly furnished unto all good works," II Timothy 3:16, 17.

"Knowing this first, that no prophecy of the scripture is of any private interpretation. For the prophecy came not in old time by the will of man: but holy men of God spake as they were moved by the Holy Ghost," II Peter 1:20, 21.

"That we henceforth be no more children, tossed to and fro, and carried about with every wind of doctrine, by the sleight of men, and cunning craftiness, whereby they lie in wait to deceive," Ephesians 4:14.

"Ever learning, and never able to come to the knowledge of the truth," II Timothy 3:7.

2. We shall either make our choice to accept Jesus Christ as Savior and Lord while we are alive here on planet earth, or we shall forever suffer the consequences of neglecting to make that choice.

"Jesus saith unto him, I am the way, the truth, and the life: no man cometh unto the Father, but by me," John 14:6.

"Neither is there salvation in any other: for there is none other name under heaven given among men, whereby we must be saved," Acts 4:12.

"And beside all this, between us and you there is a great gulf fixed: so that they which would pass from hence to you cannot; neither can they pass to us, that would come from hence," Luke 16:26.

3. We shall either go to heaven when we die, or we shall spend all of eternity in Hell/the Lake of Fire.

   "And it came to pass, that the beggar died, and was carried by the angels into Abraham's bosom," Luke 16:22a.

   "the rich man also died, and was buried; And in hell He lift up his eyes," Luke 16:22b, 23a.

   "And death and hell were cast into the lake of fire. This is the second death," Revelation 20:14.

4. We shall either look down from heaven upon the affairs of man, or we shall look up from Hell on the affairs of man.

   "And when he had opened the fifth seal, I saw under the altar the souls of them that were slain for the word of God, and for the testimony which they held: And they cried with a loud voice, saying, How long, O Lord, holy and true, doest thou not judge and avenge our blood on them that dwell on the earth? And white robes were given unto every one of them; and it was said unto them, that they should rest yet for a little season, until their fellowservants also and their brethren, that should be killed as they were, should be fulfilled," Revelation 6:9-11.

   "And in hell he lift up his eyes, being in torments, and seeth Abraham afar off, and Lazarus in his bosom," Luke 16:23c.

5. We shall either be comforted in heaven by the angels and God Himself, or we shall be tormented in Hell with the devil and his fallen angels.

   "But Abraham said, Son, remember that thou in thy lifetime receivedst thy good things, and likewise Lazarus evil things: but now he is comforted, and thou art tormented," Luke 16:25.

> *"And God shall wipe away all tears from their eyes; and there shall be no more death, neither sorrow, nor crying, neither shall there be any more pain: for the former things are passed away," Revelation 21:4.*

> *"Then shall he say also unto them on the left hand, Depart from me ye cursed, into everlasting fire, prepared for the devil and his angels," Matthew 25:41.*

> *"And the devil that deceived them was cast into the lake of fire and brimstone, where the beast and the false prophet are, and shall be tormented day and night for ever and ever," Revelation 20:10.*

6. We shall as believers either hear, well done thou good and faithful servant, and then receive rich rewards, or we shall as believers suffer great lost and suffer shame.

   > *"His Lord said unto him, Well done, thou good and faithful servant: thou hast been faithful over a few things, I will make thee ruler over many things: enter thou into the joy of thy lord," Matthew 25:21.*

   > *"If any man's work abide which he hath built thereupon, he shall receive a reward," I Corinthians 3:14.*

   > *"If any man's work shall be burned, he shall suffer loss: but he himself shall be saved yet so as by fire," I Corinthians 3:15.*

7. And would you believe that the very Word of God which so many have rejected will be the standard by which Jesus Christ will judge the quick and the dead when we stand before the Judgment Seat of Christ as believers, or the Great White Throne Judgment as non-believers?

   > *"He that rejecteth me, and receiveth not my words, hath one that judgeth him: the word that I have spoken, the same shall judge him in the last day," John 12:48.*

"I charge thee therefore before God, and the Lord Jesus Christ, who shall judge the quick and the dead at his appearing and his kingdom," II Timothy 4:1.

"For we must all appear before the judgment seat of Christ; that every one may receive the things done in his body, according to that he hath done, whether it be good or bad," II Corinthians 5:10.

"And I saw a great white throne, and him that sat on it, from whose face the earth and the heaven fled away; and there was found no place for them. And I saw the dead, small and great, stand before God; and the books were opened: and another book was opened, which is the book of life: and the dead were judged out of those things which were written in the books, according to their works. And the sea gave up the dead which were in it; and death and hell delivered up the dead which were in them: and they were judged every man according to their works. And death and hell were cast into the lake of fire. This is the second death. And whosoever was not found written in the book of life was cast into the lake of fire," Revelation 20:11-15.

CONCLUSION

I have chosen to pursue the More Excellent Way because it is exactly what I need to fulfill God's will for my life. I trust that you will prayerfully consider whether it is God's will for your life also. In closing let us unite our hearts and voices in singing to ourselves, THE CHURCH'S ONE FOUNDATION, stanza four, *LIVING HYMNS,* page 22. *"Mid toil and tribulation And tumult of her war, She waits the consummation Of peace for evermore; Till with the vision glorious Her longing eyes are blest, And the great Church victorious Shall be the Church at rest."*

AND ALL OF GOD'S CHILDREN SAID, AMEN AND AMEN!

In the Service of the King, Rev. L. D. Grant

ACKNOWLEDGMENTS

I have chosen to leave the acknowledgments until the end of this book because I wanted you to have read it before this was done. I trust that you understand now why I am so thankful to those I have mentioned.

First, I thank God who sustained me while I was writing this book. It was at His urging that I attempted to write. While I was writing it I had one continual prayer, "Lord, if there is any item in this book that doesn't please YOU, please bring it to my attention so that I may delete it immediately. And if there is any item that should be in it, and it is not there, bring it to my mind so that I may add it at once."

I also want to thank God for allowing me to travel in at least eighteen foreign countries and upon five continents. In most of these I have had the opportunity to preach and/or teach, meet people from many backgrounds, and to savor the lifestyles and foods of all. This has helped me to understand the needs of those who look to the Bible as it relates to the things of God.

Secondly, I thank my daughter, Sheila, who did the front and back covers for this book. Then my son, David, who was my computer instructor as I was writing it. Without his help I could not have typed this manuscript so that it was ready for publication.

Thirdly, I thank all those godly men who have touched my life, educated me, prayed for me, and encouraged me. I praise God for each one! I trust that this book will be a satisfying reward to them for the time and effort they invested in me.

In the Service of the King,
Rev. L. D. Grant

BIBLIOGRAPHY

AUTHORIZED KING JAMES VERSION. Grand Rapids, MI, 2000

Brown, Francis/Driver, S.R./Briggs, C.A. *HEBREW AND ENGLISH LEXICON OF THE OLD TESTAMENT.* Oxford, 1966

HARPER'S ANALYTICAL GREEK LEXICON. London and New York

Kittel, Rudolf. *BIBLIA HEBRAICA.* Stuttgaart, 1937

Liddell, Henry George/Scott, Robert. *A GREEK-ENGLISH LEXICON.* Oxford, 1961

Rahlfs, Alfred. *SEPTUAGENTA.* Stuttgart, 1962

Sholes, Jerry. *PRIMETIME RELIGION.* New York, 1979

Stephen, S. *THE ENGLISHMAN'S GREEK NEW TESTAMENT.* London

Strong, Ames. *STRONG'S EXHAUSTIVE CONCORDANCE.* New York and Nashville, 1961

Tenny, Merrill. *ZONDERVAN PICTORIAL DICTIONARY.* Grand Rapids, MI, 1963

Wykoff, George/Shaw, Henry. *THE HARPER HANDBOOK OF COLLEGE COMPOSITION.* New York, 1962

CPSIA information can be obtained
at www.ICGtesting.com
Printed in the USA
FFOW02n1111140514
5357FF